INSIDE TRUMP'S EPA

MIKE STOKER

Fulton Books, Inc.
Meadville, PA

Published by Fulton Books 2022

ISBN 978-1-63985-030-3 (paperback)
ISBN 978-1-63985-032-7 (hardcover)
ISBN 978-1-63985-031-0 (digital)

Printed in the United States of America

The cuff links pictured on the front of the book were given to Mr. Stoker upon his appointment as the Southwest Administrator of the US EPA by President Trump. Since the creation of the US EPA in 1970, all Administrators and Regional Administrators for the US EPA have been given a pair of these cuff links.

CONTENTS

PREFACE

Making the decision to write this book was no small undertaking. Not only would I be telling my story in the aftermath of a controversial firing, but I would also be telling it in the aftermath of one of the more controversial administrations in US history. Why do this, then? I decided to write *Inside Trump's EPA* for several reasons.

First, I wanted to be able to share a side of the EPA that the general public and even those who interfaced with the agency on a regular basis didn't understand. While the perception of the EPA is generally as an agency whose sole focus is on the regulatory front and playing gotcha, the enforcement and regulatory side of the EPA is actually a small amount of the work that the career men and women of the EPA do every day in carrying out the EPA's mission to protect human health and the environment.

While the EPA takes enforcement of our environmental laws and regulations very seriously, the fact is that over 60 percent of the EPA's total budget goes to grants and funding for our states, tribal nations, US territories, and even indirectly, in the Freely Associated States of Palau, Marshall Islands, and Kwajalein Atoll to implement clean air and water programs and strategies, facilitate the removal of marine debris and microplastics, protect the coral reefs, develop Brownfield projects, clean up Superfund sites, and engage in effective emergency management during federally declared emergencies. The list goes on from there. The extent and nature of the true work of the EPA will be explored in depth in this book and may belie many commonly held misconceptions about the agency.

I also wanted to write this book to pay tribute to the career staff of the EPA. My term in working as regional administrator of the

Southwest, which represents over sixty million people, covers eight times zones, and extends from Navajo Nation in New Mexico to the Northern Mariana Islands in the South Pacific, gave me the opportunity to work with the most professional and most dedicated people I have ever worked with in my life. Of particular note are the career staff in the Southwest region I worked with day in and day out. I can tell you that not once did I see a person from rank and file to senior staff who didn't give 110 percent every day they went to work.

I am also writing this book to publicly disclose actions that were taken by the top leadership in Trump's EPA that I feel did not serve the interests or directions of the administration. I don't believe the president or the senior members of the White House staff were aware of these actions. These actions didn't serve the mission of the EPA. I also believe they were unethical, violated the oath taken to serve, and perhaps were even illegal. These were actions that were taken by Administrator Wheeler, Acting Deputy Administrator Doug Benevento, and potentially, a handful of other presidential appointees.

In discussing this aspect of Trump's EPA, I feel it is important to make these disclosures so that future administrations and administrators don't repeat these actions, which would do a great disservice to the mission of the EPA and the career staff who are instrumental in carrying out that mission. Much of this book will discuss those actions, my opposition to them, and the negative consequences those actions had in serving both the administration and the EPA's mission.

When I was terminated by Administrator Wheeler, which I believe was for pushing back and opposing these actions, I made it clear as a presidential appointee that I would not discuss anything negative about Wheeler et al. until the president was out of office. I am old-fashioned and believe that when a governor or a president appoints you, you don't talk about the dirty laundry until that governor or president is out of office. I honored that commitment and waited until President Trump was out of office to undertake this project and share these thoughts with the public.

Some will say that an appointee should never disclose wrongdoings. To those, I say I vehemently disagree. By discussing the wrongs in an administration, you raise awareness in the public, in the media, and in future administrations of what took place to better ensure that history is not repeated. Indeed, even the media, which can be an incredible watchdog and bring wrongdoing by those in power to the public's attention, might learn from this book, where they could better direct their Freedom of Information Act (FOIA) requests to expose wrongful activity.

My final reason for writing this book is to provide anyone interested in the environment and its protection with an inside look at the day-to-day operations of the EPA and the vast role the agency and its employees play in making our environment safer and cleaner, improving our daily quality of life in so many ways, and protecting our human health.

I want to dedicate this book to my incredible wife, Debi, without whose persistence this book would not have been written. I also would like to dedicate this book to the career men and women of the Southwest region of the US EPA, who gave me years of working with the best of the best. This book is a salute to all of you and what you do every day in getting up and giving it your all in service to the EPA and its mission. Cheers!

INTRODUCTION

To BEGIN, I FEEL I should first introduce myself to the reader. I am a land use, agricultural, and environmental attorney who has practiced law since 1980. I have been involved in public policy and politics at the local, state, and federal levels since 1985. I have served on the Santa Barbara County Board of Supervisors, served as chairman of the California Agricultural Labor Relations Board, served as deputy secretary of state, and most recently, served as the Southwest's regional administrator of the United States Environmental Protection Agency.

Southwestern US's EPA, also known as Region 9, serves sixty million people and covers eight time zones from Navajo Nation in New Mexico in the east to the Northern Mariana Islands in the west with American Samoa, Guam, Hawaii, California, Arizona, and Nevada in between. Region 9 is the largest of the ten regions within the US EPA. In addition to serving the Pacific Island territories of the Northern Mariana Islands (CNMI), American Samoa, and Guam, Region 9 also serves 148 tribes, of which Navajo Nation is the largest.

As will be discussed in this book, I quickly became aware that all federal agencies, including the US EPA, do not give our American territories or our tribes anywhere near the attention and service they deserve. This book will hopefully shed light on this fact and will help ensure that future administrations will provide for the needs of our tribes and territories.

This book will also attempt to provide the reader with an understanding of how the US EPA functions internally. I strongly believe that the vast majority of Americans, including myself before becoming the Region 9 administrator, have no understanding of what the real EPA is all about. As an environmental attorney, my perception of the agency prior to becoming the regional administrator was completely wrong.

Like many attorneys and consultants who dealt with regulatory agencies, my assessment of the US EPA was that it was an agency whose main focus was enforcement. While the US EPA does take enforcement of our environmental laws very seriously, enforcement only makes up approximately 5 percent of the agency's resources.

I was amazed to learn within weeks of being sworn in that almost 60 percent of the agency's budget is allocated to grants and funding that serve the EPA's mission "to protect human health and the environment." From clean air and clean water projects to eliminating transboundary sewage at the US-Mexico border or cleaning up landfills and Superfund sites, the vast majority of the EPA's resources go to giving us a cleaner and healthier environment.

At the heart of this mission are the incredible career men and women who work for the EPA. The greatest honor of my professional life was the time I was given to work with the career men and women of Region 9. Indeed, the career staff in Region 9 are the most professional, passionate, and dedicated people I have ever worked with in my life. I will always be grateful to the president for appointing me to this position and giving me this opportunity. This book will attempt to pay homage to these fine individuals who get up each day wanting to make a difference, serving the EPA's mission to protect human health and the environment.

On a sad note, I will also discuss actions I believe the administrator of the US EPA, Andrew Wheeler, took that were not in the best interest of the mission of the US EPA or in the best interest of President Trump's administration. While my termination by Administrator Wheeler remains a mystery to me, I believe the conflicts and disagreements I had with him, which I will discuss in this book, were most likely the reasons that led to my termination.

Those (personal) conflicts involved actions taken by Mr. Wheeler with regard to the state of California that I believe were ill-advised. They also involved several other issues, including my advocacy for the Pacific Islands and various tribes, my persistent advocacy for the EPA to address the transboundary sewage problem at the US-Mexico border at the San Diego-Tijuana sector, and my prioritization of the uranium mine problem in Navajo Nation. On all these issues, I believe Administrator Wheeler would have preferred if I had stayed silent. I will go into much more detail in this book.

I will also explore the administrative side of the EPA and how hard it is to take on a bureaucracy of its size to make it run more efficiently. We often hear Republicans talk about running the government like a business. During my tenure as regional administrator, Administrator Wheeler would often comment on his goal and commitment to make the EPA operationally more efficient.

While I must acknowledge that the EPA made some gains in terms of efficiency through the implementation of LEAN[1] management tools, for which Henry Darwin deserves full credit at the end of the day, the EPA fell far short of becoming more efficient under Wheeler's guidance, especially with regard to reallocating resources and manpower from where they were not needed to where they were needed. Again, this book will go into much more detail regarding the lost opportunity the Trump Administration had under Administrator Wheeler's direction, to create a more efficient and responsive US EPA.

Finally, it should be noted that the contents of this book are based essentially on memory recall. When I was terminated by Administrator Wheeler at 8:00 a.m. Pacific Standard Time on February 4, 2020, my EPA cell phone was remotely disconnected twenty minutes later and my EPA laptop computer thirty minutes later, making it impossible for me to retrieve information from those sources. Likewise, I was locked out of my San Francisco and Los Angeles offices, where my personal files were located. I was never allowed to retrieve them either. Consequently, the contents of this book are based largely on events as I recall them.

In the final chapter, I will be going into much greater detail with regard to this termination and the subsequent litigation that resulted from it. While I can prove that the reason Wheeler and co.

---

[1] LEAN—Inspired by the Toyota Production System, LEAN management is a method of managing and organizing work with the aim of improving a company's performance, particularly the quality and profitability of its production process.

gave for my termination was an outright lie, I cannot prove the real reason why I was, in fact, terminated.

At the end of the day, as I think this book will, at least, demonstrate through circumstantial evidence, I was terminated for doing nothing more than my job—carrying out the mission of the EPA to protect human health and the environment. Stupid me. That was why I was told the president appointed me R9 regional administrator.

CHAPTER 1

The Road to Becoming a Presidential Appointee

AFTER PRESIDENT TRUMP APPOINTED me to be the Region 9 administrator for the US EPA, I was amazed by how many people called me thinking all it took was a simple call from me to the White House Presidential Personnel Office (PPO) to ask for a job. Folks, it just doesn't work that way. The road to becoming a presidential appointee generally occurs in one of three ways.

The first is when a cabinet secretary knows the individual and wants that individual to be a part of his or her executive agency. For instance, with the US EPA at the time the president appointed me, several of the other regional administrators had been known by Administrator Pruitt and had been sought out by him to be regional administrators. I came to the administrator's attention through the PPO with the PPO highly recommending to Administrator Pruitt that I be considered for appointment as the Region 9 administrator.

The second pathway to becoming a presidential appointee is when a member of Congress with close and strong ties to the sitting president recommends an individual for appointment to the PPO. In that situation, it is typical for the member of Congress to recommend an appointment to a specific position or just recommend the individual generally to the PPO for consideration for any positions for which the individual is qualified. Typically, in this scenario, the position the individual gets appointed to is a lower profile one.

The final pathway to becoming a presidential appointee is when the administration and PPO seek out the candidate and let that individual know the specific position for which the president is considering appointing the individual. This is the pathway typically utilized for high-level appointments, such as cabinet secretaries, undersecretaries, administrators, regional administrators, etc. This was the pathway that was used in my case.

Most individuals who are selected in this way are individuals known personally to the president or who have a long history of working for the party and, therefore, have a lot of friends in high places, such as Congress. From my years on the Santa Barbara County Board of Supervisors, as chairman of the California Agricultural Labor Relations Board, as California deputy secretary of state, and of working on the presidential campaigns of Senator McCain, Senator Romney, and Donald Trump, I was in this category. I did not seek out the administration. The administration sought me out. So when friends asked if I could help get them a job at the White House, it just wasn't that simple.

For me, it was back in May 2017 when I received a call from the PPO telling me the president was interested in appointing me to the National Labor Relations Board (NLRB). They asked if I had any interest in that position. I told the PPO that I was very interested, which launched a six-month vetting process, at the end of which, in early November 2017, I was advised that the president would be nominating me to the NLRB. While I was not assured that the president, after confirmation, would appoint me chairman, the PPO advised me that it was most likely that I would attain that position.

I will elaborate more on what took place during that six-month period, but let me first briefly explain why PPO considered me for the NLRB. In 1995, California governor Pete Wilson appointed me as chairman of the California Agricultural Labor Relations Board (ALRB). Significantly, the National Labor Relations Act (NLRA), which was passed in 1935, was made applicable to all employees with the exception of agricultural employees.

The NLRA provides employees the opportunity to organize and define their rights therein. It also defines what employers can and cannot do with regard to those organizational efforts. When there are disputes, it is the NLRB that has sole jurisdiction in adjudicating matters that come under the NLRA. The only state that provides the opportunity for agricultural employees to organize in a fashion similar to nonagricultural employees is California, which allows agricultural employees to organize pursuant to the California Agricultural Labor Relations Act (ALRA).

The ALRA, which was enacted into law in California in the early seventies, is patterned 100 percent after the NLRA. The ALRB, too, is patterned 100 percent after the NLRB. The matters and issues, therefore, that come before the ALRB are essentially the same matters and issues that come before the NLRB, except they apply to agricultural employees in California. In deciding ALRA matters, the ALRB applies NLRB decisions and precedent.

Consequently, there is no better training ground in America for a role on the NLRB than serving on the California ALRB. It was with this background that I was asked by the Bush administration in 2002 whether I had any interest in serving on the NLRB. I did, and I went through a vetting process, making it to the final round with one other individual. At the end of the day, the other candidate got the nod.

Just over twelve years later, it was now the Trump administration asking me if I was interested in the NLRB. Between April and early September 2017, I made several visits to the White House to be interviewed for the position. In early September 2017, the PPO advised me that the president wanted to move forward and appoint me to the NLRB. As all high-level presidential appointees know, it can take hundreds of hours to fill out the forms, which include ethics disclosures, financial disclosures, an FBI background check, and administration paperwork. I spent most of the month of September 2018 filling these forms out. The PPO put me in touch with the NLRB chairman Bill Gould to assist me in the process. In early October, the FBI interviewed me. By early November, the PPO told me the president was very close to submitting my nomination for appointment to the NLRB.

And then the phone call came. The individuals with whom I worked so closely at the PPO were very apologetic, but they told me the president had changed his mind. It should be noted that after my name leaked out for potential appointment to the NLRB in September 2017, a lobbying effort was pursued by lobbyists from K Street, Washington, DC. President Trump would often refer to these lobbyist groups as part of the swamp.

K Street lobbyists wanted one of their attorney friends from Washington, DC, who was well known in said swamp, to get the nod and not an outsider such as me. I was confidentially told by one member of the PPO, whose identity I will not disclose, that it was this lobbying effort that led to the president changing his mind. So much for draining the swamp.

At that point, I asked those I knew at PPO how we should move forward. They asked if I would consider becoming the director of the Federal Mediation and Conciliation Service (FMCS). While I was disappointed over the decision the president had made regarding the NLRB, after a couple of days of thought and deliberation, I called the PPO back and told them what so many presidential appointees told a president: I wanted to serve wherever the president thought I could best serve in the administration. If that was the FMCS, then I would accept that position.

So began round 2 and numerous hours of paperwork, this time for appointment as director of the FMCS. During that process, there was confusion around whether I had to undergo another FBI background check. After some back-and-forth between the PPO and the FBI, it was decided that since my prior background check had been within less than six months, a new background check and series of interviews would not be necessary. The PPO put me in contact with the Office of the General Counsel of the FMCS to fill out paperwork required by the FMCS for appointment as director. In January 2018, the president submitted my nomination to the US Senate to be the director of FMCS.

In every prior administration, the position of director of the FMCS was not considered controversial. In fact, several prominent Democrats, such as former congresswoman Lois Capps, current congressman Salud Carbajal, and Santa Barbara County supervisor Das Williams, wrote letters of support to the US Senate Committee on Health, Education, Labor and Pensions (HELP) during the confirmation process. I soon realized, however, that I was a victim of a chilling trend—what had never been controversial with prior presidents became highly controversial with President Trump.

In mid-January 2018, I was advised by the PPO that the Democrat minority staff for HELP had advised the White House that they would invoke the cloture rule with regard to my nomination. Invoking cloture requires that the Senate allocate thirty hours of Senate floor time to debate the nominee after the nominee has been passed on for confirmation by the committee—in this case, the HELP committee. In other words, had they pursued the nomination process, the Senate would have had to spend thirty hours debating me. If that isn't a waste of Senate time, I have no idea what is, but that's the way cloture works.

From what I know, prior to the Obama administration, cloture was hardly ever invoked. In the first eighteen months of the Obama administration, Republicans invoked cloture just over ten times for different nominees. In the first eighteen months of the Trump administration, cloture was invoked over one hundred times. This is a sad and dangerous precedent that hopefully the Republicans will not repeat with the Biden administration.

In any case, the PPO, having been advised that cloture was inevitable, informed me that with so many people waiting for confirmation, who also had cloture invoked on their nomination, it would take up to two years for my nomination to go through the Senate. With that reality before us, my contacts at the PPO said they would start looking for high-level positions that did not require Senate confirmation.

In January and February, I had several calls with the PPO discussing various possible appointments. Nothing came of any of those calls. Then in March, the PPO called and asked if I had any interest in serving as regional administrator for Region 9 of the US EPA.

My initial response was, "Of course! But how would we get around the cloture rule?" To my shock and surprise, the appointment of a regional administrator for the US EPA does not require Senate confirmation. To this day, I can't believe that with all the positions that do require Senate confirmation, these key EPA positions do not. The reason for this was because the US EPA, believe it or not, was created by an executive order by President Richard Nixon and not created through an act of Congress. Significantly, that executive order provided for the ten regional administrators of the US EPA to be appointed by the president without senate confirmation.

Accordingly, it was this executive order that established the parameters for the agency and for congressional interface with the agency. One of those items of interface was having regional administrators who would not be subjected to Senate confirmation. So while appointing thousands of, frankly, mediocre board, commission, and executive agency positions requires Senate confirmation, appointing one of ten regional administrators essentially responsible for enforcing and implementing the environmental laws and regulations of the United States requires none. Upon learning this, one of my first thoughts was, "Why wasn't this our first port of call?"

Within a week, Administrator Pruitt's chief of staff, Ryan Jackson, called me up to do an initial interview on the phone. That interview led to me flying to Washington, DC, for what was, in essence, a rather perfunctory, in-person interview with Administrator Pruitt and Chief of Staff Jackson. In that interview, I advised them that I was definitely interested in the job but that I wanted my duty station as the regional administrator to be in the Los Angeles field office for Region 9 as opposed to the headquarters located in San Francisco, California.

Pruitt and Jackson said that wasn't a problem, and the decision was made then and there that I would be the next appointed Region 9 administrator. Jackson then introduced me to the EPA White House liaison, Charles Munoz, to start the processing procedure.

There were those who opposed the president and who attempted to use my duty station as something controversial. In the world of politics, you create controversy for a presidential appointee wherever you can based on the premise that if you embarrass the presidential appointee, you embarrass the president. Hence, there were those who jumped on my duty station, hoping to make it a controversial issue.

However, the Southern California Field Office (SCFO) for R9 actually makes a lot of sense being the duty station for any R9 RA who intends to be in the field the vast majority of the time. The fact is, the SCFO is located in Southern California, which has the largest concentration of underground fuel tanks in the US, is just north of the US-Mexico border with the transboundary sewage issues at the San Diego-Tijuana sector, has three times the amount of Superfund sites than San Francisco within seventy-five miles of the office, is within fifteen miles of the Port of Los Angeles / Long Beach where 40 percent of the nation's imports enter the US and where EPA conducts inspections to intersect knockoff pesticides and motor vehicles that do not comply with EPA standards, and is located where twenty million people reside, which is one-third of the entire population of the territory R9 covers.

The reality is, if the EPA were created today, the headquarters for R9 would not be San Francisco but Los Angeles. If I needed to be in San Francisco, I would be in San Francisco. If it didn't matter what physical office I had to be in, I would be in the SCFO with video capability to videoconference with anyone in EPA, whether from HQ or San Francisco or the other two R9 field offices in San Diego and Honolulu.

I will discuss in much more detail the nuances involved in a presidential appointee and the location of their duty station in a subsequent chapter. As discussed in my interviewing process, I was hired with the understanding that I intended to be a regional administrator who spent very little time in my office and the majority of the time on the road with the stakeholders involved with EPA Region 9 issues. I knew this could mean anything from visiting Superfund sites, consulting with my emergency responders, or visiting my 148 tribes or Pacific Islander territories.

Whatever pressing Region 9 issues were on hand, I believed my presence in the field would make me an abundantly more effective administrator than if I were sitting behind a desk in San Francisco. And significantly, not only did Jackson and Pruitt tell me they were 100 percent behind my request during my interview to place my duty station in Los Angeles, but they also made it very clear that a condition to being hired was my willingness to travel throughout my region and being regularly in the field.

As it turned out, I interviewed with Administrator Pruitt and Chief of Staff Jackson the week before all hell broke loose with Scott Pruitt and his personal issues, which the national media attacked him for. When Pruitt and Jackson said I was hired, they told me there was no problem with Los Angeles being my duty station. Once everything hit the fan with Pruitt, however, Jackson advised me they would have to lay low on the appointment and the reassignment of duty stations until the Pruitt situation blew over. They didn't want the designation of a regional administrator's duty station to become another hot topic issue Pruitt would have to address. I fully understood, concurred, and waited for my appointment and the assignment of my duty station.

Over the next two months, more and more issues involving Administrator Pruitt became public, and the controversy only escalated. It became clear to me that if I were to wait for the issues involving Pruitt to disappear before being appointed, my appointment would most likely never happen. Consequently, in early May, I called Chief of Staff Jackson and told him to make San Francisco my duty station. I suggested we could monitor my travel over the first six months to clearly establish that it wouldn't matter whether my duty station was in Los Angeles or San Francisco. Jackson asked me if I was comfortable with this arrangement, to which I replied yes. I asked Jackson, if the facts bore it out, if he would give me his assurance to redesignate my duty station as Los Angeles six months later. He said yes. As a result, I told him to appoint me so that we could move forward and I could get to work.

On May 18, 2018, I was appointed as the eighteenth regional administrator for Region 9 of the US EPA, never thinking my duty station would be an issue. I only looked forward to my new position. I took the mission of the US EPA seriously and was intent on protecting human health and the environment for Region 9 and its sixty million people, who were scattered throughout multiple time zones. As I will be discussing in a subsequent chapter, I had no idea that the selection of a duty station or being a regional administrator who believed in being in the field versus in an office could become such controversial issues. But then I was living in the world of politics, where often nothing made sense.

To be continued.

CHAPTER 2

The First 100 Days (Part 1)

With my duty station agreement in place with Chief of Staff Jackson to initially be San Francisco, I was processed in a relatively short period of time to be the next Southwest administrator for the US EPA. Six weeks prior to the formal appointment, Jackson put me in touch with the acting Southwest administrator, Alexis Strauss, to coordinate the transition.

For the reader's benefit, the EPA has acting and regional administrators in the ten regions. An acting regional administrator is a career EPA employee who holds the position pending the appointment by the president of the regional administrator. The acting administrator is always a career employee and is usually someone with the highest seniority. In Region 9, that was definitely Alexis Strauss. Ms. Strauss had worked for every Region 9 administrator since the creation of the agency, going back to the seventies. During my tenure at EPA, I came to admire and respect Ms. Strauss more than any other career or political employee in the agency.

I spent the six weeks prior to my formal appointment going over process issues with Ms. Strauss. During that time period, she introduced me to Ms. Amy Miller, who could also assist me with issues of which I needed to be aware. (At the time, Ms. Miller was acting as Strauss's chief of staff.) Finally, the time came for the appointment. The actual appointment by the president was made on May 18, 2018, which fell on a Saturday.

Consequently, my first formal day on the job and a ceremonial swearing in would take place in San Francisco on Monday, May 21, 2018. On Sunday night, May 20, 2018, I boarded a flight in Burbank for San Jose and overnighted there and made arrangements for Ms. Miller to pick me up at seven o'clock on Monday morning and drive me into the Region 9 headquarters in San Francisco.

Week 1

The next morning, Ms. Miller picked me up promptly at seven o'clock. Prior to that time, I had not personally met Ms. Miller, so the drive into San Francisco was the first time we were able to personally meet each other and discuss a path going forward. During that conversation and in the months to come, I came to have great admiration and respect for Ms. Miller.

Upon arriving at the San Francisco office, I was escorted to my personal office and was met by Ms. Strauss and, for the first time, Ms. Deborah Jordan, who had been acting as Ms. Strauss's deputy director. Ms. Jordan had served previously as director of the R9 Office of Air and Radiation (OAR). Strauss, Miller, and Jordan were all career EPAs. Shortly thereafter, Charles Munoz, who had processed me in for employment by EPA in the DC headquarters two months earlier, joined us as well.

Kenneth Wagner, who had been appointed by Administrator Pruitt as special adviser for Regional and State Affairs, was also there. This position was a new position created by Pruitt, which, among other responsibilities, made him a key point person between regional administrators and the administrator. In other words, if a regional administrator had issues or concerns related to that regional administrator's dealings with headquarters, Wagner provided clarity.

As will be discussed in subsequent chapters, I believe Wagner's position is a critical one that future EPA administrators should keep, but they should carefully consider who is appointed. When Wagner left his position, Wheeler never embraced it the way Pruitt had, and the void he filled interfacing between headquarters and regional administrators was lost. I also believe this void was a key reason why I was ultimately terminated by Wheeler.

In any event, Ken Wagner was also there to greet me and assist me through my first two days. As part of his position, Wagner made it a point to meet all regional administrators at regional offices on their first day and spend the first couple of days with the newly appointed administrator to help them in the transition.

At approximately 8:30 a.m., I was sworn in. After going over HR processing issues, I attended my first senior staff meeting at 10:00 a.m. A typical Monday for an RA in Region 9 is a weekly senior staff meeting at 10:00 a.m., followed by a weekly EPA headquarters' senior staff meeting at 11:00 a.m. This meeting involves the administrator, the administrator's chief of staff, the deputy administrator, and all assistant administrators stationed in Washington, DC, and takes place in the headquarters' green room. The regional administrators participate by video from their regions unless they happen to be at the headquarters on any given Monday.

While most senior staff meetings focused on the substantive issues facing the region of which the division director wanted to make all the senior staff aware, this senior staff meeting was essentially an opportunity for me and for the senior staff to introduce ourselves and for us to have an open question-and-answer dialogue. In my mind, our first encounter couldn't have gone any better. In retrospect, that first meeting was the beginning of a process that would, in a very short time period, lead me to conclude that my expectations of what career men and women at the EPA represented couldn't have been further from the truth.

I had a feeling many of them entered the meeting with a certain set of expectations of me too and left the meeting dumbfounded to learn that their new RA was a guy who attended seventy-six Grateful Dead shows while Jerry Garcia was still alive and was a Trump Republican who was clearly passionate and committed to serving the EPA's mission "to protect human health and the environment."

Following the R9 senior staff meeting, I went to my personal conference room to participate in my first EPA HQ Monday senior staff meeting. The meeting was fairly routine with Administrator Pruitt introducing me and many of the senior staff welcoming me to the EPA. We then went around the regions for a regional update of what would be coming up in the next week.

When Administrator Pruitt called on Region 9, I reported that I would be giving my first all-hands to Region 9 the next day, that I would be a keynote speaker on Wednesday at the annual meeting of the California Agricultural Commissioners and Sealers Association, that I would be in the LA Field Office (SCFO) on Thursday and Friday to introduce myself personally to the SCFO staff, and that I would have a videoconference call with the governor of Guam and a meeting with Wayne Nastri, executive director of the South Coast Air Quality Management District (SCAQMD).

I also reported that the following week, I would be headed to Kīlauea in the island of Hawaii, also known as the Big Island, to assess EPA's response to the volcano eruption. This volcano had become a federally declared emergency with FEMA and would bring specific emergency mission assignments to our agency that EPA would carry out.

The conference call ended, and I spent the rest of the day going through processing for HR issues, receiving a couple of briefings from the staff, and speaking to Ms. Strauss regarding her recommendations for who should be named my chief of staff (COS) and the deputy regional administrator. I then reviewed notes I had prepared for my first all-hands speech, which I would give the next day. My first day on the job ended with meeting Ken Wagner for dinner to discuss several things, including my upcoming appointments.

From the six weeks that I dealt with Ms. Strauss before being appointed, I came to have a great deal of admiration and respect for her candor and knowledge of the agency. She also became someone I already trusted on day one, more than any other political appointee with the agency. This was really an anomaly. Generally, those who are politically appointed will stay in their own lane and trust only those who share the lane to have their back. In my case, what was becoming my normal would be the exact opposite.

For instance, the way Jackson was handling the relocation of my duty station caused suspicion, but it was Strauss who was well aware of my duty station issue and kept it in focus. So on day one, my duty station issue was a priority for her. She worked tirelessly to ensure we provided Jackson with documentation he needed to honor his commitment to me and change my duty station to SCFO. In her documentation, Strauss made it clear that a duty station in the SCFO for an R9 RA was inconsequential. Bottom line is, actions speak louder than words. By noon on day one, I could settle into my job and focus on tasks at hand knowing Strauss had my back more than Jackson did.

To wrap up day one, Strauss, Jordan, and Miller walked into my office and asked if they could have a word. "Of course," I said. While standing, they all proceeded to share with me their belief that I had been treated unfairly throughout my process into the agency and to assure me that they were fully committed to making sure all i's would be dotted and t's crossed to ensure that Jackson would have no reason to say no after the six-month waiting period. These three were becoming my port in a brewing storm.

After my dinner with Wagner the night before, I knew that not only did he have my back but that we would also be friends after our respective jobs ended. The wild card that I couldn't get a read on was Munoz, and boy, would my suspicions be confirmed down the road.

It would become a common occurrence for Strauss, Jordan, and Miller to engage in frank discussions with me regarding issues that they believed those opposed to the president would potentially attempt to use against me. In politics, opponents to a president do whatever they can do to embarrass a presidential appointee on the theory that if you embarrass the appointee, you embarrass the president.

Some of these discussions included alerting me to the harsh reality that the media would be out to get me as a result of being a Trump appointee. As a result of this relationship that was developing, these three women would soon be known to me as the Big Three.

They promised to review every aspect of my schedule, scrutinize my meetings, and pursuant to EPA guidance policies run all travel plans through the EPA travel office in Cincinnati for final approval.

They told me that regional administrators in the Trump administration received an unprecedented amount of Freedom of Information requests from reporters wanting to see the RA's calendar and travel schedule and meetings with everyone they met on EPA business. They told me to expect the same thing, but they assured me they were there to make sure I did everything by the book. By the end of the day, I truly believed these three had my back, and nothing ever happened to cause me to change that assessment. On the contrary, that assessment was only proven more to be true. As for the FOIA, I was told that by my departure, over two hundred FOIAs had been submitted requesting information pertaining to me.

This assessment was important, as my last meeting on day one in the office was with Ms. Strauss to discuss her recommendations on who my deputy regional administrator (DRA) and my COS should be. I told Ms. Strauss that obviously, the DRA job was hers if she wanted it. She declined and said she intended to retire upon the new administrator being appointed, and as previously stated, she would stay on to be special adviser to the regional administrator. She strongly recommended that Deborah Jordan be appointed as DRA and that Amy Miller be appointed as my COS. With that, the meeting came to an end, and she left for the day.

At dinner, Mr. Wagner quickly became Ken, and we began reviewing my all-hands for the next morning. He made some recommendations regarding style elements, but as far as substance was concerned, he liked it. Ken took another moment to reiterate how well he thought the first day had gone. I then told him that it was my intention to appoint Jordan as my DRA and Miller as my COS.

We discussed that some in HQ would question my appointing a career as COS. The fact was, all other RAs had appointed political appointees as their COS. There was no question that I would be breaking with the precedent. I told Ken that I knew it would be controversial to some but that I fully trusted Miller, and my intuition of people was generally spot on, and my assessment of Miller was that she was someone who fitted perfectly with my personality and style.

I also told Ken that I thought it would send the right message to the career staff of R9 that one of their own colleagues was my COS. Ken said that he had no problem with it and that I had to go with my gut feelings on the issue. The dinner ended.

The next day, I arrived at the office around 7:00 a.m. My all-hands was scheduled for 10:00 a.m. I met with Strauss first to tell her that I had decided to follow her recommendations. Jordan, who was flying that day back east, would be notified of her new position via voice mail. The next task was to ask Miller into my office where, in person, I could ask if she would be my COS. To this request, her answer was, "It would be an honor." Miller's acceptance officially launched the Big Three, and they would remain in that role until Strauss retired in August of 2019.

During my tenure as the R9 RA, I would continue to defy the norm of all the other RAs who appointed politicians as their COSs. All my COSs would come from the career pool within Region 9. I initially appointed Ms. Miller as my COS, and when I appointed her as R9's enforcement division director, I appointed my tribal division director, Laura Ebbert, as my COS.

When I appointed Ms. Ebbert as the R9's division director for the newly created division of Tribal, Intergovernmental and Policy Division (tribes, borders, Pacific Island territories, NEPA, and environmental justice), I then appointed the SCFO director Steven-John Leonido as my COS. In all three cases, career staff for R9's EPA would be my COSs.

I was on my way downstairs to the auditorium, where all-hands was held. I looked around the room, and I quickly realized that in attendance to meet their new RA were roughly four hundred career staff of R9 EPA. I felt my chest rise with pride and was quickly humbled by this honor. Ken walked to the podium, said a few words, and then introduced me as Region 9's new RA.

My first remarks were to drill home the point of my availability to each and every employee. I wanted each person sitting in the room to realize I was there for them and their team to help the EPA succeed with our mission statement. I wanted every career staff member to know they could contact me personally anytime. Just like each employee's, my email address was easy to figure out, and they would always receive an answer back from me. (All EPA email addresses are last names with a period followed by the first name and @epa.gov.)

I went on to explain that I would be an RA who met the problems head-on in the field. I would also reward hard work and success in person, not while sitting behind a desk. As the Region 9 administrator, I was their voice, liaison, and advocate to relay their needs and wishes to the headquarters in Washington, DC. I then shared with them my new appointments from that morning, to which I received a round of applause.

I ended by saying that Jerry Garcia's ties were my ties of choice, which received another applause, and I concluded by saying that their biggest fault was probably being Giants fans since we all knew the Dodgers were the better team. This comment produced expected loud hisses and boos, and I broke out into laughter.

I hung around to personally meet and greet my people before running upstairs to the nineteenth floor to grab my briefings and head to the airport. The next day, I would be in Ontario for the CAAG commissioners' meeting in Lake Arrowhead.

An event worth noting happened on my drive to Lake Arrowhead with Miller. My phone was on speaker as I took the call from the assistant administrator of the EPA Office of Air and Radiation (OAR), Bill Wehrum. It's a story worth telling, which I will circle back to in much more detail in the chapter "EPA versus California."

My final two days were spent in the SCFO, where I got to know many of the SCFO staff. It also gave me the opportunity to get to know the SCFO staff director, Steven-John Leonido, whom I would come to build a very trusting relationship with and whom I would eventually name him last COS. Other than that, it was routine meetings, a telephone call with the governor of Guam, and staff briefings via VTC to San Francisco.

Week 2

On week 2, I was off to Hawaii. Upon my arrival at the airport in Honolulu, my new COS, Miller, was already there. When I landed, she picked me up in a rental car to start our week at the Kīlauea emergency operations center in Diamond Head. I was briefed by FEMA and the state of Hawaii's officials and attended their daily morning briefing.

Off record, several folks in the ops center told me of their concern with Hawaii mayor Harry Kim, who had refused to enforce a mandatory evacuation order. He was letting residents come and go as they wanted to their homes. I didn't give much thought at the time to what they were telling me. Within two days, that would dramatically change.

We were then off to meetings with the governor of Hawaii, meeting with R9's Honolulu Field Office (HFO) career staff, and meetings with Bruce Anderson and Keith Kawoaka of the state of Hawaii's Department of Health. In Hawaii, the state health department also has the responsibility of overseeing enforcement of environmental laws. This can be different in each state. In California, it is CalEPA; in Nevada, the Nevada Division of Environmental Protection; in Arizona, the Arizona Department of Environmental Quality. In American Samoa, it is the American Samoa EPA; in Guam, the Guam EPA; and in Northern Mariana Islands, the Bureau of Environmental and Coastal Quality.

I assessed from my meetings with Hawaii state officials that they appreciated EPA's emergency management but were frustrated with the mayor in regard to the mandatory evacuation issue. They also brought something to my attention and requested my possible intervention. Part of the EPA's emergency management mission assignment from FEMA was establishing air monitoring stations throughout the island to monitor not only overall air quality but also potentially deadly H2S vapors being airborne from the volcano.

I believe that at the time, we had twenty-one monitors up and running, providing all emergency responders real-time air quality results every eighteen minutes. These folks asked me if the EPA could provide that information to the public on our R9 EPA website. I discussed it with my COS, and the answer was definitely yes, but upon our inquiring about the issue, we learned that for whatever reason, the emergency responders were operating under the premise that Mayor Kim had stated that he did not want that information to be made public, as it could be misinterpreted by the general public.

I told Miller that we needed to set up a conference call with Strauss, Jordan, and my R9 Superfund and Emergency Management Division director, Enrique Manzanilla, to discuss the air monitoring situation. My first meeting with the HFO career staff was just like my first meetings with my SF HQ and SCFO career staff. The meeting couldn't have gone any better.

From that meeting, an issue was brought to my attention, which I would play a critical role in addressing. The HFO was housed in a Hawaii state building. Upon entering the office, I felt like I had gone back in time to the fifties. The office was designed in a bizarre way, and it did not take advantage of the limited space they had. The office was dark with very little natural lighting, and the furniture looked like it was more than thirty years old.

At the end of the meeting, I told them they deserved better. I made it clear that they deserved what their colleagues had in SF or in the SCFO or the San Diego Field Office (SDFO). I told them I would do whatever I could to have the HFO either moved or significantly improved. This was something that I would continue to advocate for over the next two years, and I am proud to report that just prior to my termination, I learned that it was agreed between HQ and the General Services Administration that the office was going to be completely renovated within six months with a plan that the HFO staff informed me they would support and be very appreciative of.

As of the time of writing this book, I have no clue whether those improvements were made during the pandemic, but I can assure you, once COVID-19 is over, the fine people working in the HFO will have the field office they all deserve to call their duty station.

So back to the end of the day. My COS and I returned to our hotel and got on a conference call with Strauss, Jordan, and Manzanilla to discuss the issues regarding EPA's role in the volcano response. I told them that it was outrageous that the mandatory evacuation order was not being taken seriously by the mayor. That was something that didn't involve the EPA, but I did say EPA should take unilateral action to put our air monitoring data on our website for the public to have real-time information.

I felt strongly that the air quality data should be made available to the general public. When accurate data is available, the public has a right to that information. You may not be aware, but in most places in the United States, you can go on a website and see that your local air quality district is providing information for you to find out the status of the air you are breathing.

For instance, where I live in Carpinteria, California, I can go on www.ourair.org, which is sponsored by the Santa Barbara County Air Pollution Control District, to receive current air quality conditions. What I was trying to do in Hawaii was the exact same thing. I wanted to give the local residents the current status of their air quality, which I knew EPA could provide in real time with updates every eighteen minutes.

Back to the conference call. Manzanilla, whom I had only met in my senior staff meeting the week before, aggressively pushed back, essentially advocating to not get involved. At the time, his approach caused me to wonder if he was the one senior division director whom I could not count on to support me in pursuing my priorities and agenda.

In any event, we ended the conference call with Strauss and Jordan suggesting that the diplomatic approach would be for me to contact the state officials I had met with and suggest that the state of Hawaii make a request to FEMA that FEMA give EPA a mission statement to put the air monitoring information on the R9 website. We ended our call, and I told Miller how appreciative I was for Jordan's and Strauss's continued efforts to help me accomplish my goal through appropriate protocols.

I called Hawaii's state officials. During this call, I proceeded to explain that a request to FEMA from the state would probably solve the problem. When I hung up, I wasn't sure if they would make the call. The politics of the situation was this. The governor was up for reelection and was running against a fellow Democrat. The race was very close. No one wanted to cross the mayor, as his endorsement could be key in a very close race, hence the hesitancy by the state officials on my suggestion that they make the call to FEMA. They clearly would have been much more comfortable with EPA just taking the action unilaterally with the air monitoring situation.

The next morning, Miller and I caught a six-o'clock flight to the island of Hawaii. When we arrived, we were picked up by one of R9's emergency responders and went to the hotel where our folks were staying. Heading up our emergency management at the time was on-scene coordinator (OSC) Steve Calanog, whom I met for the first time in a hotel conference room.

Also present was a Coast Guard Strike Team that had been assigned to the response and were working directly with our team. US Coast Guard Strike Teams that are deployed in an emergency management situation are incredible people who do incredible jobs in federally declared disasters.

Our meeting went well. I advised them of the call I had the night before with state officials regarding our air monitoring data, and we discussed the crazy situation with the locals being able to come and go to their homes in the mandatory evacuation designated areas. They told me later on in the day during my tour that I would see firsthand how the mandatory evacuation wasn't being taken seriously by local residents.

I ended that meeting and headed to the 10:00 a.m. emergency ops center meeting with all the emergency responders. Before discussing that meeting, I would be remiss if I did not mention something about Steve Canalog. In my meeting with my staff and the Coast Guard Strike Team, Mr. Canalog seemed lukewarm at best to me. I am pretty good at reading body language, and the body language of Steve said, "This is a Trump appointee I am not going to like, and I'll give him the respect he deserves as the R9 RA, but that's it."

Throughout my tenure, our first meeting in Hawaii would evolve into the first of many meetings centered on federally declared disasters. By the time of my termination, I had also spent time with Steve on the ground in the Northern Mariana Islands where Super

Typhoon Yutu devastated the area and in Paradise, California, where the Camp Fire literally burned the entire town to the ground.

I never mentioned my initial gut feelings with Steve about our first meeting until I was writing this book. However, through these disasters and my overall advocacy for emergency responders, by the time I departed, I believed Steve felt that of all the RAs he had worked with, I was one he was most appreciative of for the support I provided to our emergency responders. I left the EPA feeling that Steve and I had developed a strong bond and respect for each other. Steve would confirm that fact in our discussion after my departure. More on this subject in the upcoming chapter on emergency management. Back to the island of Hawaii.

We arrived at the ops center, and I participated in the briefing. After the meeting, the individual heading up the FEMA efforts on the island—his name I can't recall—came up to personally thank me. "Thank me for what?" I asked. He said, "For helping break the deadlock with the mayor and the issue of the EPA air monitoring data that the emergency responders had access to but not the public."

I asked him what had happened. He went on to say that FEMA had received calls from state officials the night before requesting that EPA post the air quality data information on our public website and that he had just received word that FEMA would be sending a mission assignment to EPA to do exactly that. By the end of the following week, the website was up and running. It was available to anyone in the public to see exactly what the emergency responders were seeing.

Back to the mayor. He was at the Emergency Ops Center. I recall the look he gave me from across the room. If looks could kill, that would have been my last day working for the EPA. I made a judgment call to not go and introduce myself personally. We had reached out previously to have a meeting, and he put our folks off. So we proceeded to the staging area where I was to meet some of my folks and other emergency responders from other agencies for my tour.

Everywhere I went, I made it very clear that as a former Santa Barbara County supervisor who had been involved in local disasters with mandatory evacuation parameters, mandatory evacuations were just that. Once you left your home, you were not allowed to return to your home until the order was rescinded. In other words, I made it very clear to everyone I spoke with that I fully disagreed with the mayor's decision.

We proceeded to go and tour the air monitoring stations and evacuation centers, then we walked to within a couple hundred feet of the volcano's lava flow. The flow was very erratic, erupting every one hundred yards with lava flow. Some eruptions went hundreds of feet in the air. Then the penny dropped, and I saw what I was warned of earlier that morning.

Between where we stopped to be safe and the live lava flowing, a couple of locals were riding their bicycles wearing shorts and flip-flops with no shirts. One was within twenty to thirty feet of the lava flow. *Unbelievable*, I thought. But these were the rules in place at the time of this mandatory evacuation.

The tour ended, and my COS and I returned to the airport to fly back to Honolulu. The next day was routine with more routine meetings, but it was also not routine on another front. State officials who two days earlier had expressed their disappointment with regard to the mandatory evacuation order, or lack thereof, advised me that the mayor had changed his mind.

After the emergency ops meeting where I had been given the look by one miffed mayor, the mayor gave the green light to all the emergency responders that the mandatory evacuation order would now become real. I believe all local residents were given seventy-two hours to go back to their homes to get whatever they needed, and thereafter, anyone going into the area closed by the emergency evacuation were subjected to arrest. What a change a day can make. In this case, it was for the good.

On the flight home, I felt a sense of accomplishment. It was starting to sink in that an EPA regional administrator could be a major player and could really make a difference. When I flew to Hawaii EPA, EPA could not share our air monitoring data with the public, and local residents were allowed to ride their bikes literally right up to the lava flow. By the time I landed back home, a real mandatory evacuation order was in place; and within five days, our air monitoring data was on the R9 website for anyone to view. Week 2 was over. Week 3 would be off to Arizona.

Week 3

The following Tuesday, I arrived in Phoenix. This was a special day for me. I was going to tour the Rio Salado with Senator John McCain. I was fairly close with the senator from the days he campaigned for me when I ran for Congress in 2000 and from having served on his presidential executive committee when he ran for president in 2008. I was thinking how cool it would be for the senator to see his old friend now serving as the Southwest administrator of the US EPA, and I was there in my capacity as the regional administrator to help him with his Rio Salado project.

The Rio Salado, also known as the Salt River, runs through the counties of Gila and Maricopa and is the largest tributary of the Gila River. The river is about 200 miles long. Its drainage basin is about 13,700 square miles large. The largest of the Salt River's many tributaries is the 195-mile Verde River.

The river once naturally flowed, but with the development of Phoenix, it had been turned into large drainage basins to handle stormwater runoff in heavy rains. Essentially, an incredible natural marvel had been turned into drainage basins to protect Phoenix from flash floods.

The senator, Arizona State University, and numerous major players from Arizona decided several years ago that it was time to return the river back to the gem it once was. It was a commitment they believed they owed to future generations of Arizonians. Senator McCain stated, "The Rio Salado project has the potential to transform the Salt River bottom and realize an untapped valley treasure."

R9 had been providing funding to assist in moving the project forward. I would soon find out that my invitation to tour the Rio Salado was not just for the senator to see his old friend and tour a project that R9 was assisting with. No, it was to persuade me to become a strong supporter of the project and to urge HQ that the EPA supported the Rio Salado becoming the twentieth Urban Waters Federal Partnership (UWFP) project.

When I arrived in Arizona, I didn't even know what a UWFP project was. That would soon change. What I would soon find out was that being a UWFP list was a game changer. Once the project was on the list, many more doors opened for federal funding.

Anyway, back to the tour. I arrived early in the morning at a designated field base operations at Phoenix Sky Harbor International Airport. I was to meet the senator and his chief of staff for the tour. Upon arriving, I met with his COS but was saddened to hear the senator couldn't make it.

At that time, Senator McCain had been fighting cancer, and he was having a bad health day. The tour would be left to his COS and another member of the project. I didn't know it, but I would never see the senator again, as he would pass away three months later on August 25, 2018. (RIP, my friend. You were a patriot, served your country so bravely in the Vietnam War, and represented the best of what a public servant is.)

The helicopter took off, and we spent an hour and a half touring the Salt River project from one end to the other. Upon landing, we went to a Salt River project status update at Arizona State University. All the partners involved with the project were there to give an update. I was introduced to most of the major partners, and the ask I heard over and over was, the Rio Salado needed to be added to the UWFP list.

The meeting ended. We then went on a land tour of several portions of the project, stopping at two tribal lands—what you may call tribal reservations—to visit with tribal members and discuss their roles in the project. The Rio Salado ran through both of these tribes' land. The meeting also served a second purpose for me. I had made representing my 148 tribes one of my personal RA top priorities. I made a pledge that I would do my best to visit all 148 tribes. I would be visiting my first two tribes on this trip to Arizona. By the time I left the agency, I can proudly say, I visited almost sixty tribes in just twenty months for an average of three tribal visits a month.

The day ended, and I went back to my hotel to prepare for meetings the next day with the director of the Arizona Department of Environmental Quality (ADEQ), Misael Cabrera, and his staff. There were some hot-button items involving the state of Arizona and EPA, and the meeting was an opportunity for us to introduce one another and to start the dialogue involving these issues. As for the UWFP, I had decided before the Rio Salado land tour ended that I would make having the Rio Salado listed in the UWFP a personal priority going forward.

For the next twenty months, I attempted to persuade HQ, with a strong focus pointed in the direction of the assistant administrator for the Office of Water, David Ross, to add the Rio Salado. Two weeks before I was terminated, I was told by Mr. Ross that the Rio Salado was officially the twentieth project of the Urban Waters Federal Partnership. When I hung up, I envisioned that big smile of Senator McCain looking down at me with him giving his famous thumbs-up.

The next day was going to be my first meeting with the director of ADEQ, Misael Cabrera, and his staff. I have a great deal of respect for Director Cabrera. He was as firm in representing his position and the state of Arizona as I was in representing the interests of the EPA. In the beginning, our mutual desire to see the transboundary sewage problem eliminated at the US-Mexico border helped create a strong, mutually respectful relationship.

It should be noted that most of the attention in this book and from Congress in regard to the transboundary sewage problem at the US-Mexico border has been at the San Diego-Tijuana sector. However, in Arizona, there is a significant problem in Naco and Nogales that has largely gone ignored and does need to be addressed by Congress.

In any event, from the outset, our relationship started out on a very positive note as a result of this issue. Over time, as a result of issues that the state of Arizona and EPA were not on the same page about, our relationship cooled off. One issue was the state wanting to extend the current Motorola Fifty-Second Street Superfund Site in

Phoenix to West Van Buren, which had been remediated as a separate site by the state.

They initially requested EPA not to list West Van Buren as a Superfund NPL site, allowing the state to take responsibility for remediation. However, by the time I was sworn in, the state, after years of being the responsible party, changed course and now wanted the EPA to take it over as a federal Superfund site, allowing the state to be off the hook.

Another issue was air quality nonattainment problems due to dust in Maricopa County. There was also the proposed Rosemont Copper, which, if approved, would be the largest-producing copper mine in the world, and the state wanting to assume Section 404 powers of the Clean Water Act. By the time I left the EPA, the state had advised the EPA and Director Cabrera had advised me personally that the state would not be pursuing assumption powers of Section 404 of the Clean Water Act, a decision I personally supported given the opposition by the tribes located in the state of Arizona.

Three weeks before my termination, I was in Arizona for a major announcement regarding the new Waters of the United States Rule (WOTUS). Director Cabrera attended that event. There, he publicly stated to those in attendance that I was doing an incredible job. He would always mention my advocacy regarding Arizona issues and the fact that in just under two years, I had been to Arizona over seven times while my predecessor from the Obama administration was only in Arizona once in seven years. (I have no idea whether this assertion is true or not.) This trip would be my eighth and final trip to Arizona representing the EPA.

Bottom line is, while Director Cabrera and I had our disagreements, I had as much respect for him on my last day on the job as I did from the very outset. That respect would start to develop from the meeting we had the next day. Director Cabrera and I met the next day and covered many issues. The first issue on his agenda was to display his LEAN board and what had been accomplished while implementing LEAN.

I will discuss LEAN later as it relates to the EPA. However, keep in mind, as previously mentioned, the EPA's LEAN accomplishments were from the dedicated work of Henry Darwin. Henry, prior to being appointed to Trump's EPA, served as the director of ADEQ, Cabrera's predecessor, and he was the one who started the LEAN process with ADEQ prior to his departure. Again, more on LEAN and the EPA later.

During our meeting, we discussed the transboundary sewage issues with Nogales and Naco. I told Director Cabrera that addressing transboundary sewage along the entire US-Mexico border was going to be one of my top personal priorities as RA. We then focused on the lawsuit Arizona had with the International Boundary and Water Commission (IBWC).

We discussed an upcoming meeting we would be having in Nogales the following week referred to as Border 2020, which included the major stakeholders involved with border issues, and we discussed a meeting we would have at the ADEQ office with EPA and DOJ to discuss potential settlement of the IBWC lawsuit. DOJ was in the meeting because they represented the IBWC in the lawsuit. More on this lawsuit in my recap of week 4, but at this point, let me just briefly say that the lawsuit was based on Arizona's position that the IBWC had been derelict in their duties to address transboundary sewage problems as required by Congress when they created the IBWC. I left believing the meeting couldn't have gone better.

The next morning, I arrived at the San Diego Border Office (SDBO) at eight thirty. At nine, I met the staff. The first person I met with was the director of the SDBO, Hector Aguirre. I would become very close professionally and develop a huge amount of respect for Hector. He will unquestionably be a division director for Region 9 sometime in the future.

After meeting with the staff, the two of us talked about the transboundary sewage issue. As in my assurances to Director Cabrera the day before, I assured Hector that addressing this issue would be one of my top personal RA priorities. I believed we hit it off so well, because Hector was also passionate about addressing the transboundary border sewage problem, and he was happy he had a new RA who was making that issue one of his top priorities, and I was happy because I could sense immediately that I had a director of the SDBO who was all in when it came to helping me address this personal priority.

We then discussed a meeting I would be having with Mayor Serge Dedina, the mayor of the city of Imperial, to discuss the transboundary sewage issue. Mayor Dedina arrived, and he was escorted into the SDBO conference room for us to get acquainted.

I feel as if Mayor Dedina and I had an instant connection. He is the mayor of a beach town and is a surfer. I come from a beach town in Carpinteria, California, and am an ocean swimmer. We both have an incredible respect and love for our ocean. His community had been hit the hardest by the transboundary sewage issue. While numerous stakeholders in the San Diego area had made eliminating transboundary sewage a top priority, the mayor had been the most active and passionate, given that his community was being hit the hardest.

As the meeting ended, the mayor said he had never felt so optimistic that the issue would finally be taken seriously by the EPA. As I write this book, whether we hit it off so well because we were both all in for initiatives that would give us cleaner and healthier oceans or because we would both be perfectly happy if all business meetings could take place in flip-flops, shorts, and a Tommy Bahama shirt, I will never know. But one thing I do know is, the residents in the city of Imperial Beach should be aware that they have a great advocate and representative in Mayor Serge Dedina.

I will write more about this later, but as a result of the advocacy and efforts of Mayor Dedina, myself, and other stakeholders, by the time I was fired from my position at the EPA, Congress had appropriate $350 million to the EPA to clean up the sewer issue at the San Diego-Tijuana sector of the US-Mexico border.

Before ending week 3 and heading home from San Diego, an unscheduled event was added to my calendar. Early that week, while I was in Arizona, an emergency management was developing in the City of Coronado, California. Some nutcase had been taking switches apart for disposal. These switches contained mercury vials. He had disposed of the nonmercury portion of the switches but not the mercury vials. He had allowed those mercury vials from the switches to pile up in his garage, and then a fire broke out in his garage.

The Coronado Fire Department arrived, and as they were extinguishing the fire, they noticed a silvery sheen on the water. The silvery sheen was mercury. Once discovered, the Coronado hazardous materials team was dispatched. Coronado, at the time, contracted a private company to provide hazardous materials work for the city. The County of San Diego called our emergency responders for R9 and gave us a heads-up that the R9 emergency management team might be getting a call to respond, and they were right.

The next morning, our EPA's emergency management folks were called, and the essence of the conversation was that due to responding to the fire in the City of Coronado, the majority of the City of Coronado's emergency management budget had been used up in response to the mercury fire. This was money they would have paid the private contractor with. They requested the R9 emergency management unit to take over the operation.

We dispatched a small team. They were there by Tuesday and by Friday. The R9 unit was essentially in the final stage of cleanup. Upon arriving in San Diego, a tour of the site and lunch with the on-scene coordinator (OSC) had been added to my schedule. The OSC was Michelle Rogow.

We had a very pleasant lunch, and while discussing the recent response, I asked if she had any pressing issues that I should know about to make her job better and more responsive. She stated that she felt that previous R9 regional administrators didn't give emergency management the support it needed or deserved and that she hoped I would be more supportive. Hopefully, by the time I left, I hadn't let Michelle down.

As for lunch, it was another example why I strongly believe RAs should be more field oriented than office oriented. You can get a lot more out of a lunch with one of your OSCs in the field where an emergency management is taking place than having the same brown bag lunch in your office on the nineteenth floor of the R9 headquarters in downtown San Francisco.

So in the first three weeks, I had been to two emergency managements. The first was the Hawaii volcano, which was a federally declared emergency with FEMA mission assignments given to EPA, and the second was an emergency management caused by a crazy guy who had decided to keep mercury vials piled up in his garage, causing a fire that in the end depleted a city's emergency management budget. My quick takeaway was that emergency managements can come in all shapes and sizes with all kinds of variables that can impact a huge range of people from hardly anyone to thousands and thousands of people.

This was a good learning curve for me and was also the beginning of my ever-increasing respect for our EPA emergency responders and the work they do. When I started with EPA, I had no idea what their needs were; but by meeting in the field and asking questions, within months, advocating for those needs became one of my top priorities.

I headed back to my hotel room, where I would begin preparing for my second keynote speech to be given as the R9 administrator. This keynote speech was with the California Independent Petroleum Association (CIPA). Many attendees knew me from past professional positions I held. My speech went well, and upon my termination, within the next two years, I had given over one hundred more in-person keynote speeches. As I traveled to the airport to fly home for my one day off that week, I was looking forward to my next week, when I would be given the opportunity to meet the other nine regional administrators.

Week 4

Actually, I wouldn't get an entire weekend off. I flew back from San Diego on Saturday, drove home, and arrived in my garage early that afternoon. I threw on a pair of shorts and a Tommy Bahama shirt and met up with friends for a relaxing late afternoon. On Sunday morning, I was back in the car and driving to LAX to catch my flight to Chicago for my first RAs' meeting.

As previously mentioned, Ken Wagner was the special adviser to the administrator for the Regional and State Affairs. As part of his interfacing with the RAs and their regional needs, he would also have quarterly meetings where we could all meet to discuss common issues, needs, complaints, etc. This kind of interfacing is critical when you consider the placement of each RA and the totality of the job. Ken understood this, and bringing us all together quarterly only made each RA better in their position.

This would be my first opportunity to meet the other nine regional administrators and contribute to the meeting regarding my region, and later in the week, Ken would join me to meet with ADEQ and DOJ to discuss the Arizona IBWC lawsuit. I remember when Mayor Dedina said that he believed I was the first EPA political person he had met who was serious about the transboundary sewage issue. I believe he was trying to thank me for my commitment and to underscore the fact that I was the first R9 RA who was all in on the issue for the long haul.

Mayor Dedina had already known there was one other political in EPA who was all in, and that person was Ken Wagner. From my research and from everything I was made aware of Ken, he was the first person in the EPA to believe the transboundary sewage problem should have been an EPA national priority. I was the second, and I believe David Ross, the AA for the Office of Water, was the third. Thankfully, Congress became the fourth, and now it is a congressionally mandated EPA priority.

Back to the first RA meeting. We discussed LEAN and its implementation, and we discussed the newly proposed EPA reorganization plan. While I was largely supportive of the plan, I was opposed to one aspect pertaining to enforcement at the US EPA. At the end of the day, my perspective prevailed in the final reorganization plan that the US EPA implemented.[2] We had a conference call

---

[2] In the original recommendation provided to Administrator Wheeler, Acting Deputy Director Henry Darwin had recommended that the "enforcement" division be eliminated and the function of enforcement be absorbed in each of the respective offices or divisions. For instance, enforcement attorneys would be part of the Office of Water to enforce Clean Water Act violations. Enforcement

with Henry Darwin to get his input regarding LEAN, and I got to know my colleagues from the other nine regions.

The meetings were wrapping up, and most of the RAs caught flights back home, but a couple of us for one reason or another stayed over to board flights the next day. On my calendar, I was scheduled to fly out the next day to Phoenix, where Ken and I would meet regarding the IBWC lawsuit. That evening, I had dinner with Ken to discuss our upcoming meeting in Phoenix. Just like our dinner in the San Francisco office, I was very impressed with Ken's choice of wine. It's a known fact that Ken is quite the connoisseur of fine wines.

The next day, it was back to Phoenix for me and Ken. This was the second time in two weeks that I was in the state of Arizona. The next morning, Ken and I met with the attorneys representing the

---

attorneys in the Office of Air and Radiation would enforce Clean Air Act violations. At the time of the recommendation, the ten regions were essentially split. Half the regions, like Region 9, had a stand-alone enforcement division. The other half of the regions pursued their enforcement actions through the respective divisions. I believed Region 9 had provided a role model for how a stand-alone enforcement division could work. I also believed a stand-alone enforcement division proved to be much more efficient and also proved to help better accomplish compliance goals.

Before Acting Deputy Director Darwin presented his recommendations to Administrator Wheeler, I had advised him I did not personally support the recommendation. All regional administrators were asked for our respective opinions. I believe I was the only regional administrator that was on record as being opposed. Several other regional administrators said they would "prefer" the stand-alone enforcement division but did not formally oppose the recommendation. All other regional administrators supported the recommendation. When Administrator Wheeler announced his decision, he advised us that he supported the stand-alone enforcement division. The position I had advocated for prevailed. I'll never know if my sole opposition with the initial recommendation was the beginning of the top brass in headquarters starting to wonder whether I was the right guy for the job in Region 9. What I do know, I was asked my opinion and I gave it. Had the initial recommendation been adopted, I would have done my job to implement whatever Administrator Wheeler directed. And I would have done it without voicing opposition or questioning the decison. As mentioned throughout the book, I never publicly voiced my opposition to anything Administrator Wheeler did while President Trump was still in office.

IBWC. We went over the case and the reasons that the DOJ clearly believed the state of Arizona's lawsuit had no merit. I had already concluded as much while reviewing the pleadings and the law. There was no question that the transboundary sewage issue had not been addressed by the federal government.

It was easy to blame it on the IBWC, because the IBWC was created by Congress to address the problem. However, the bottom line is, the IBWC can only fix problems that Congress gives them the money to address. And at that point, Congress had appropriated the IBWC very little to address the transboundary sewage issue. But what was on the table was more important than Arizona wanting to blame the IBWC for the lack of a response.

Congress had previously appropriated $21 million for Nogales and its sewage treatment infrastructure to respond to transboundary sewage. The hitch was, the money had to be committed to the project by the end of 2018, or it would be lost. Through all the finger-pointing, nothing had been done. Additionally, in the lawsuit, the DOJ was also taking the position that the city of Nogales was in default of their share of the contribution to operate the existing facility. As for the $21 million appropriation from Congress, to get the $21 million, Nogales would have to come up with the additional $5 million match.

From my perspective at that point, Nogales was essentially just ignoring the issues and leaving it to the state of Arizona to fight their battles for them. I phoned Director Cabrera after our first meeting the week before to suggest that we could all work to help Nogales with their match but that the state had to put more pressure on Nogales to accept their realistic share.

By the time of my departure from the EPA, I would come to agree with Arizona and many of the stakeholders in San Diego that the IBWC had definitely been more the problem than the solution when it came to addressing the transboundary sewage problem at the border. However, as far as Arizona was concerned, the city of Nogales was much more the problem than the IBWC.

With the city of Nogales being so unreasonable, I suggested to Misael that we could potentially put off for another day what the proportionate share of responsibility for operating the Nogales sewage operations was between IBWC and Nogales. If Arizona would drop their lawsuit to show their good faith to the DOJ, we could focus on the $5 million we needed to come up with over the next couple months to match the $21 million federal on the table. I told Cabrera that Arizona could always refile their lawsuit later with nothing lost, but if the parties continued to be adversaries, we would lose the $21 million, and then everyone would lose. I suggested all this to Cabrera conceptually, as I had no idea how the DOJ would approach the problem.

We met that morning, and we laid out our strategy. DOJ would take the lead. I planned to jump in when appropriate and give my take. In the meeting, I told them that from my week before and my phone conversation, I truly believed Director Cabrera wanted to resolve this issue. Politically, he couldn't just cut and run and leave Nogales to deal on their own with the federal government, but he did not want to lose the $21 million on the table.

We arrived at the ADEQ offices and met for an hour and a half. I thought the meeting went well. I played my cards at the appropriate time, and we left with the DOJ saying they would look at options to pursue their claim against Nogales at a later date if we would look at options to come up with the $5 million match.

There were a lot of other smaller details that each party needed to assess and see what options we each had. We left with the DOJ and Arizona still adversaries but with a framework that could potentially lead us to a positive resolution. My whole focus was, we couldn't lose that $21 million currently on the table.[3] That afternoon, Ken

---

[3] Thanks to the efforts of Jonathan Brightbill, former acting assistant attorney for US Department of Justice and the attorney who was representing the United States and the International Boundary and Water Commission (IBWC), my efforts to get the state of Arizona to dismiss the lawsuit with prejudice was successful. Mr. Brightbill could have played hardball given how the city of Nogales was responding, or their lack thereof. But he didn't act just as an attorney doing his job. He, like me, knew how important the $25 million was for Nogales in responding to transboundary sewage issues.

When Nogales failed to respond or assume responsiblity, he went beyond the call of duty to allow the state to step up to the plate to assume responsiblity

and I departed in Ken's rental car for Tucson. We would overnight in Tucson and then leave the next day for our Border 2020 meeting in Nogales.

What is Border 2020? The Border 2020 program is an environmental program implemented under the 1983 La Paz Agreement. It builds on the Border 2012 environmental program, which emphasized regional, bottom-up approaches for decision-making, priority setting, and project implementation to address the environmental and human health problems of the border regions.

In November 2019, AA of OITA, Chad McIntosh; myself; and other representatives of the US EPA and of Regions 6 and 9 met with our counterparts from Mexico to discuss the framework of a Border 2030 program. In those meetings, I was successful in getting Mexico to add marine debris removal and water beneficial reuse to Border 2030's program framework. That framework was to be finalized in 2020, but with COVID-19, it was put on hold. When the Border 2030 program is finally adopted, I hope the new administration will assure that the topics of marine debris and water beneficial reuse remain as environmental goals and policies Mexico will commit to. Anyway, back to Border 2020 and our meeting.

For obvious reasons, transboundary sewage was the key issue with the stakeholders involved in our Border 2020 meeting in

---

for finding the $5 million that needed to be put on the table to get the $20 million match. As previously mentioned, I had committed some US EPA dollars toward that match to help the state of Arizona. Jonathan could have refused to approve the $20 million match without the city of Nogales agreeing to the share of responsibility for dollars already spent. But he didn't. He approved the money being allocated with only the state agreeing to come up with the $5 million match with a dismissal of the lawsuit without prejudice. The people of Arizona, especially the citizens, deserve to give Mr. Jonathan Brightbill a big thank you from my dealings with the city officials representing Nogales that probably won't happen; but the residents of Nogales have a right to know exactly who you can thank for the $25 million being allocated.

On July 14, 2021, the IBWC awarded a $13.8 million contract for the repair of more than five miles of the crumbling pipeline that transports sewage from the US-Mexico border in Nogales to a treatment plant in Rio Rico. The contract covers phases 1, 2, and 3 of the project.

Nogales. Not much of substance was on the agenda for this meeting. It was more an update on projects that were taking place. The issue of transboundary sewage came up, and the representative of IBWC spoke. The IBWC had been waiting for a new commissioner to be appointed by the president. That would happen the following October with the appointment of Jayne Harkins. More about that appointment later.

I can't remember who spoke on behalf of the IBWC, but I remember a pessimistic report with an attitude that said, "Don't expect much." I remember thinking that IBWC wasn't here to be part of the solution but, in fact, clearly, to be part of the problem. As stated earlier, they rely on Congress for appropriations; and if Congress doesn't appropriate funds, they have no money to allocate.

Having said that, I am a glass-is-half-full kind of guy, and I take pleasure in finding solutions to problems, not finger-pointing, and the guy speaking on behalf of IBWC was definitely a glass-is-half-empty or maybe glass-is-completely-empty guy. Anyway, when it was my turn to speak, I just emphasized that we could all make excuses, or we could all agree to work together to get the best we could.

I made it clear that I wasn't going to make excuses, that addressing the transboundary sewage issue would be one of my top priorities, and that I would do everything I could to protect the environment and human health from transboundary sewage problems with whatever resources I was given. I made it very clear that once I left the meeting, being out of sight and out of mind was not an option for me.

I concluded by verbally committing to work with all the stakeholders to come up with new and innovative approaches to resolve the problem. One of the several suggestions I made was for the stakeholders to consider forming a 501(c)(3) nonprofit that could accept donations from philanthropists and environmental advocacy organizations. Having been a strong advocate of private-public partnerships during my tenure as a member of the Santa Barbara County Board of Supervisors, I saw this issue as having great potential for a private-public partnership to address transboundary sewage, especially at the San Diego-Tijuana sector of the US-Mexico border.

Director Cabrera then stood at the podium and thanked me for my comments and then shared with those in attendance that I had been to Arizona twice in my first four weeks on the job but that my predecessor visited the great state of Arizona only once in seven years. I will say it again. A lot gets accomplished when you meet the problems head-on and face-to-face in the field and not sitting behind a desk. Now may be a good time to throw in a friendly reminder of the Big Three having my back.

I think you are starting to understand the extent of the schedule I kept throughout my tenure at the EPA, and the big three continuously went through my schedule with a fine-tooth comb to assure that every trip I took was 100 percent in full compliance with the EPA travel guidance policy. Additionally, they strictly scrutinized all my outreach efforts to assure there would never be merit in the countless Freedom of Information Act requests submitted by the media regarding my travel and my meetings.

Week 4 was coming to a close, and I was successful in placing a strong focus on what would become well known and highlighted as one of my top personal priorities: responding to the transboundary sewage issue. Week 5 would be my first opportunity to personally meet the people representing the Pacific Island territories and to help lay the foundation for my other personal priority: my advocacy for the Pacific Island territory issues and for the wonderful people who resided there.

CHAPTER 3

The First 100 Days (Part 2)

Week 5

I FLEW TO SAN Francisco on Monday, the eighteenth, landed early, and took an Uber to the SF office, where I would start my day with meetings and briefings. There was a flurry of business taking place throughout the entire building. The San Francisco office would be hosting the annual Pacific Islands conference. In attendance would be representatives from American Samoa, Guam, Northern Mariana Islands (CNMI), and the Freely Associated States, which included Palau and the Marshall Islands.

The conference would run from Monday to Thursday, and I was looking forward to my time with this group of people on Tuesday and Wednesday. These were people I would come to know well in advocating for their interests, and they were people I would come to consider my lifelong friends.

On Tuesday morning, my Pacific Island staff, Alexis Strauss, and my COS, Amy Miller, walked me down to a large conference room where all the attendees were located. I would give a welcoming address. Before getting into the details, let me briefly fill you in regarding the annual Pacific Islands R9 conference. In even years, the meeting is traditionally held in June in San Francisco at the regional headquarters building. In odd years, one of the territories or Freely

Associated States (FAS) hosts the conference. In 2018, it was San Francisco. In 2019, Guam would be hosting the conference.

As I entered the room, I saw people moving around freely and talking with one another, as the meeting had not yet been called to order. I entered and began circulating to introduce myself to as many attendees as possible before the meeting began. John McCarroll, my Pacific Islands director, came to my side and quietly let me know it was time to begin. John started the meeting with all the proper, formal introductions, and now it was my chance to address the crowd.

I began by thanking each and every one for attending our annual meeting. I made sure to draw attention to the distance many of them traveled to attend our conference. I then proceeded to give my opening remarks focusing on Pacific Island territories' people and their needs, and I promised to make the Pacific Island territories one of my top personal priorities.

I stressed that I was looking forward to my first trip to one of the territories in August, to American Samoa. During that trip, I would be attending the annual US Coral Reef Task Force meeting. Later in the book, I will dive deeper into the working aspects of the Coral Reef Task Force.

I concluded my speech as I did with my Region 9 staff in my first all-hands—by telling them that I was available to any of them 24-7. With that, I ended with giving them my personal cell number and reminding them of my EPA email address.

John recessed the meeting for twenty minutes so I could spend personal time with the attendees and get to know them better. I want to take this moment to emphasize my developing working relationships. Director McCarroll and I shared a passion for the Pacific Islands, and through my time with the EPA, we worked harmoniously to ensure that the Pacific Island territories' needs began to be met. Just to be clear, I am referring to basic needs, such as clean air and water, needs we take for granted.

When I touched base with my Pacific Island territory staff later in the day, they told me the meeting exceeded all expectations. The attendees had an informal reception planned for five o'clock that night at a local restaurant. I was not initially invited. My staff wanted the attendees to feel comfortable and enjoy themselves, and they had no idea whether they would be comfortable with the new R9 RA present. This reception was not about me but them. However, shortly after the opening session, the attendees approached my staff and asked them to invite me to their reception.

The word I got back was, they liked what they heard and would be honored for me to attend. I accepted their invitation. I spent some quality time at the reception and really got to know some of the attendees and left the reception knowing that once again, my gut had not led me astray. This group of people from the Pacific Islands were very special people who had been ignored by previous administrations.

I made a personal commitment to myself as I walked back to the office from the reception. Ignoring the Pacific Island territories' needs and interests was not going to happen again, not on my watch. I would make sure that while I was the RA, they would get what they deserved, nothing more and nothing less.

The next day, I hit the ground running and completed my portion of the Pacific Island meetings. Some of the attendees for the conference that week included Ameko Pato, the director of American Samoa EPA; Walter Leon Guerrero, the director of Guam EPA; Eli Cabrera, the director of CNMI Bureau of Environmental and Coastal Quality; and Roxanne Blesam, the director of Palau EPA. When you take a close look at what these four individuals have done in their positions with such limited resources, it is mind-boggling. I was so impressed by their tenacity and passion for carrying out their respective missions.

Three of these individuals would become very good friends, but one, sadly, would not. Ameko Pato tragically passed away during my trip to American Samoa. His deputy, Fa'amao Aselele, would become his replacement, a very close friend of his. I met Ameko in San Francisco, then on the tarmac as he picked me up at the airport in American Samoa. Tragically, the last time our paths crossed was at a barbecue held in my honor to honor US R9 EPA and American Samoa EPA.

I will share more of this trip in the last section of this chapter. But I want you to know that Ameko will always be one of my heroes based on where American Samoa EPA was prior to him becoming the director and where he took American Samoa EPA as director. More on that to follow.

The rest of the week was filled with several briefings by my staff. Briefings are not discussed much in my recaps, as I feel the reader would find these briefings very boring. However, I believe I had almost two hundred briefings in the first one hundred days. That fact even gives me cause for pause. The week ended with a very important meeting between myself and my FEMA R9 counterpart, Bob Fenton.

I would come to know Bob well in the upcoming federally declared emergencies—Super Typhoon Yutu in CNMI, the Camp Fire in Northern California and Paradise, and the Woolsey Fire in Southern California. Both of these fires occurred in the month of November 2018. However, that was still five months away. It was a good introductory meeting, and we both left the meeting with the understanding that we would call the other if we ever needed any assistance from the other. Five months later, those calls would be forthcoming on a regular basis.

With the meeting over, I headed to San Francisco International Airport to catch a flight home. Week 5 was over, and week 6 would take me back to DC for meetings in headquarters, meetings with members of Congress, including meeting with Minority Leader Nancy Pelosi, and a very important event to attend in Region 9.

Week 6 would end with me participating with Administrator Pruitt in the signing of the Record of Decision (ROD) for the Casmalia Resources Superfund Site, an event that meant Casmalia was in the last five years for Superfund listing. It was a big event for me, as I was the elected county supervisor from Santa Barbara County who took the action in 1991 to have the EPA list Casmalia as a Superfund site in the first place. Things do come full circle.

Week 6

On Monday morning, bright and early, I boarded a plane set for Washington, DC. On Tuesday and Wednesday, my schedule was filled with meetings that included several at HQ to meet with many of the associate administrators to discuss some of our mutual R9 issues. This trip also offered the first opportunity to get to know one another better. Since becoming the RA, they had only known me by videoconference. Now we would have the chance to meet one another in person.

On Wednesday, I would meet with my home district congressman, Salud Carbajal. This meeting allowed us to touch base for the first time after my RA appointment. I was also scheduled to meet with Minority Leader Nancy Pelosi. This would also be our first meeting since my RA appointment. One of my talking points for the Pelosi meeting was to discuss the Superfund NPL site at Hunters Point.

Hunters Point was an old naval base located in San Francisco, situated across from where the Giants' old Candlestick Park was once located. Months before my appointment as RA, Hunters Point had become very controversial, especially for the EPA. During my first days on the job, my staff briefed me that Hunters Point was one of EPA's hottest issues in our region. To summarize the issue at Hunters Point, here is what Wikipedia states.

> As of August 2020, the former shipyard site is still being decontaminated, and has been split into multiple parcels to allow the Navy to declare them clean and safe for redevelopment separately. While developer Lennar has built and sold hundreds of new condominium units in the SF Shipyard development of the property, a number of regulators, activists, and cleanup workers have claimed that the site is still heavily contaminated and the Tetra Tech, the company contracted to handle cleanup and testing, has repeatedly vio-

lated established cleanup protocols, deliberately falsified radiation test results at the site to falsely show that there is little remaining radiation, and fired employees who attempted to force workers to perform radiation tests as required.

According to an article published in 2017, the Navy stated that at least 386 out of the 25,000 plus soil samples that have been collected over the past two decades were identified as "anomalous." The first residents began moving into homes in June 2015. In September 2016, the US EPA halted the transfer of additional land at Hunters Point from the Navy to the city and to real estate developers.

By the time I was sworn in as RA, two representatives of Tetra Tech had been indicted for criminal fraud and would later, in June of 2019, plead guilty and be sentenced to prison for falsifying testing results. In June of 2019, the DOJ sued Tetra Tech for false billing as a result of falsifying soil and building test data and sought reimbursement of the $280 million that the navy had paid Tetra Tech for testing. (Ironically, I had first advocated for the DOJ to take this legal action in June 2018.)

With this backdrop, I was going to meet with Leader Pelosi, who had made dealing with Hunters Point one of her local top priorities. (FYI, Hunters Point was located in Pelosi's district.) As a result of Tetra Tech having so many contracts directly with the EPA for soil testing, the narrative had become that EPA was in bed with the navy. This was not a good narrative for the EPA to have.

By the time of my meeting with Pelosi, I had already laid out a proactive and transparent course of action to be followed by R9 staff. I toured the site a couple of weeks earlier to personally assess the situation from the ground. I then met Leader Pelosi and assured her that I would not let the navy make the decisions going forward and that the EPA would take the lead regarding sufficient testing protocols. EPA would do everything possible to work with the navy, but the situation now called for more aggressive follow-up of independent testing than would normally be required. As a result, I would stand firm that the navy follow the protocols the EPA would be requesting to be followed to assure that the public was not at risk.

For the parcel of land that condominiums had been built, I would request that the state of California's Department of Health (DOH) and Department of Toxic Substances Control (DTSC) independently test the site. I would also designate one of my senior advisers to attend every residents' association meeting of Hunters Point going forward to ensure that they had direct contact with me and with representatives of the EPA. I assured Leader Pelosi that I was firm in wanting to hold Tetra Tech 100 percent accountable for their actions.

I also said I was hopeful the navy would take legal action not only to be reimbursed the hundreds of millions of dollars paid for testing to date but also to seek damages for the extra work that would now have to be undertaken going forward to assure the public that Hunters Point posed no health risks. Leader Pelosi's COS, Robert Edmonson, was in the meeting, and I told him to call me anytime 24-7.

I ended the meeting with the suggestion to Leader Pelosi that she consider hosting a meeting in San Francisco when she was in the district with EPA, the navy, several representatives of the residents, and DOH and DTSC present. I suggested this could be a good opportunity to keep the pressure on the navy to do the right thing. Leader Pelosi thanked me and said she concurred with my course of action and believed I had the situation as much under control as possible given the history of what had transpired to date.

One month later, Leader Pelosi hosted the meeting in San Francisco, which went according to the strategy we discussed. Shortly upon returning from the DC trip, I received a letter from her addressed to my San Francisco HQ address dated June 28, 2018.

Dear Mr. Stoker:

It was a pleasure to meet with you during your visit to the United States Capitol on June 27th.

Many thanks for your commitment to the cleanup and transfer of the Hunters Point Naval Shipyard. Your work to ensure public health, hold a transparent process that engages the public, and holding Tetra Tech accountable is critical and greatly appreciated.

Thank you again, Mike, for your leadership.

Best regards,
Nancy Pelosi, Democratic Leader

That letter would be hung on the wall in my San Francisco Office and remain there until the week I was fired. With the meeting concluded, it was off to the airport to catch a flight to LAX and rent a car to drive to Santa Maria, California. The next day, I would be signing the Record of Decision (ROD) to be the last chapter in removing Casmalia from the Superfund listing.

On June 28, I arrived at the Casmalia Superfund site for the signing of the ROD with Administrator Pruitt. The signing was scheduled for 10:30 a.m. I knew the site well. In 1991, as a member of the Santa Barbara County Board of Supervisors, I put Casmalia on the board agenda with the request that my colleagues approve sending a letter to the US EPA requesting that they list Casmalia as a Superfund site.

Casmalia had been operating as one of two Class I toxic waste sites in California. The other site, which is still open, is the Kettleman Hills Hazardous Waste Facility. As a Class I site, it could take the worst of the worst toxic chemicals. For years, it was believed that impermeable clay underlined the entire Casmalia site, making leakage of toxic chemicals into the groundwater supply impossible. By the late eighties, substantial evidence was proving just the opposite.

By 1989, the Casmalia toxic waste dump was closed. By 1991, I was wanting to see the EPA take it over as a Superfund site, which would assure that it would get the attention it deserved in terms of remediation. By 1993, Casmalia had been listed as an EPA Superfund NPL site. Now twenty-five years later, I was about to sign the documents as the RA of R9 to provide the final chapter for delisting the site that I had requested as a county supervisor to be listed under Superfund status.

Upon arriving in Casmalia, I found it odd that I had to go through a security gate and that only a limited number of media had been invited. This was an event that the administrator was attending, so consistent with EPA protocol, the public affairs department at HQ handled all details, including the invite list. (At an event that only I attended as the RA for R9, the public affairs department from R9 would handle the matter.) When I inquired as to the limited invite list, I was told that HQ wanted a very controlled event since the administrator had been under siege in the national media over various controversial issues that had arisen over the past three months. I thought, *It is what it is.*

Pruitt arrived, and we got into a Suburban to take a tour of the site. In 1990, the water ponds on the site were reddish gray and reddish brown. There was very little vegetation. The site literally looked like something on Mars. On this day, it was very different. The ponds were clean and thriving biologically. Indeed, the EPA Superfund team that focused on real remediation and a true restoration of the site back to its original condition had accomplished their mission once again.

Our tour ended, and we were escorted to a table under a tent where both Administrator Pruitt and I would sit. I would begin with opening remarks and then introduce Administrator Pruitt. I opened with comments summarizing how personal this event was for me and then introduced the administrator. Administrator Pruitt first thanked the EPA, the contractors, and all the stakeholders for a job well done by the EPA. He then thanked everyone who came to attend the event. He then sat down and signed the pertinent documents. The delisting process had begun. It was another success story in the world of EPA Superfund sites.

We left and drove to Orcutt to a restaurant that was a favorite among locals, which twenty-five years earlier had been one of mine too. The restaurant was called the Far Western. It was originally located in Guadalupe, but a new Far Western had been built and was being operated in Old Town Orcutt. For those of you visiting the Santa Maria area, I highly recommend you try the Far Western and the Hitching Post, which is ironically located in the town of Casmalia, a small town of 144 residents, and sitting just over a mile away from the gates that take you to the Casmalia toxic waste site.

Enough with fun facts and walking down memory lane. The reason for coming to the Far Western was to have a lunch meeting upstairs with Central Coast agricultural leaders. The meeting was special to me. As a county supervisor, I quarterly hosted an agricultural leaders' luncheon at the Guadalupe Far Western. Now I was meeting with them as the RA of R9. Again, things can and do come full circle.

The meeting went well. I made some comments, Administrator Pruitt made some comments, and then most of the meeting was open dialogue. I saw that Pruitt was feeling very comfortable in this setting. He had been taking unprecedented political heat, but for an hour and a half, he hung out with people who appreciated him and appreciated his agenda. I felt like if his HQ staff and I didn't have to say it was time to go, he would have stayed there all day. He had been given a short but sweet reprieve from the outside world of politics.

We got up and said our goodbyes, and it was off to fly up to the San Francisco office. Pruitt was to meet with my senior staff the next morning, followed by a meeting with CARB chairman, Mary Nichols, to discuss the fuel economy standards rule, which would be discussed in the next chapter. By seven thirty that night, I would personally experience why Administrator Pruitt was living on edge from the political heat that was out to have him removed as administrator.

At 7:30 p.m., I received a call from one of Pruitt's assistants saying there had been a breach of confidentiality. Given the meeting the next day, we had changed the administrator's schedule for an earlier arrival time. My recollection was, he would arrive at 7:30 a.m. instead of 8:00 a.m., as originally scheduled. That change had been decided around 6:00 p.m. We updated all my senior staff, as they would be attending to meet with the administrator.

Within an hour of alerting my staff of the change, an environmental activist group that had protested outside the San Francisco

HQ building the day I was sworn in and that had been active in calling for Administrator Pruitt's resignation posted the administrator's new arrival time on their website. In other words, what only Pruitt, his staff, myself, and my senior staff knew was now known to the world.

On their website, this group was calling for their own to be at the R9 San Francisco office no later than 7:30 a.m. to protest Administrator Pruitt. To this day, I have no clue who leaked that information, but I have my suspicions. What I do know is, neither Pruitt nor I leaked that information, and I don't believe any of Pruitt's staff who accompanied him on the trip had leaked that information. That left my senior staff. I'll just say that when I see that person in the future, I will ask him, and I have a feeling he will attest to the fact that he was the culprit. I guess I will leave it at that for now.

We had made arrangements for the administrator to arrive from a side entrance and not the main entrance the next morning. The entry went fine. No one had figured it out, and the administrator was brought into the building and up the elevators to the nineteenth floor to meet with me and my senior staff. The meeting went well, and then Pruitt left to meet in another conference room with Nichols. I did not attend that meeting and was never told by Pruitt how the meeting went.

Immediately upon the Nichols meeting ending, I left with the administrator, his security detail, and my COS to go down the elevators and take the administrator out through the same side entrance that he entered. One of the people on his security detail stated he was concerned as the protesters had discovered where the administrator was exiting and would be outside the side door waiting. The administrator had to exit and cross the sidewalk to reach the Suburban that would take him to San Francisco International Airport.

I could see the concern in Pruitt's face. He almost turned white on the spot. What he was going through was what he had been going through every day for the last three months. I would not wish on my worst enemy what Administrator Pruitt had to contend with day in and day out during that period. I spoke up and told his security detail that I knew these protesters and that as we exited the door, they would be to our immediate right. I suggested that my COS and I divert to the right to allow us to interface with the protesters. That would allow the administrator to run straight into the car waiting for his arrival.

His security person asked, "Are you really okay with doing that?" I said absolutely. Administrator Pruitt looked at me and said, "Are you comfortable doing this, Mike?" I confirmed I was. His security person told the administrator, "I think it will work." We opened the door, and my COS and I bolted right and cut off the protesters as they came straight at us. It was a relief to see, out of the left corner of my eye, the administrator's Suburban jetting down the street, safely on its way to San Francisco International Airport. That was the last time I would ever see Administrator Pruitt.

Week 6 was over. After helping get Administrator Pruitt out safe and sound, I was on a plane myself bound for home. Week 7 would bring a big surprise that I can say was not at all unexpected. By the same time that next week, Administrator Pruitt would resign, and the president would name Deputy Administrator Andrew Wheeler as acting administrator for the US EPA.

Week 7

Week 7 was short and sweet. I was in the Southern California Field Office (SCFO) on Monday and Tuesday. On Wednesday was the Fourth of July. On Thursday, I was teleworking from home when I received an email alert on my EPA phone. Administrator Pruitt had resigned. On Friday, the EPA political appointees would have an all-hands with the newly named acting administrator, Andrew Wheeler.

Before talking about the Wheeler all-hands that took place the next day, let me say a couple of things about Administrator Pruitt. Notwithstanding the fact that he had been his own worst enemy with some of the things he had done, I liked how he personally interfaced with me. He seemed to care about my recommendations for issues involving R9 and was a guy who would not have done anything in my region without first advising me and getting my opinion. As for his successor, the man just named acting administrator, he would end up being just the opposite.

The next chapter regarding EPA versus California will get into that fact in great detail. What I can say about Administrator Pruitt is this. I met him twice in person. I met him first when I interviewed with him and his COS, Jackson. I then met him again on his trip to California the week before he resigned. In our weekly Monday videoconference with HQ, he was very personable and probing of each of the RAs' regional reports.

Wheeler? In short, I never found him personable. He never really seemed to interface with his RAs. In almost two years, I only had three one-on-one conversations with him. My other RA colleagues told me they all experienced the same thing, and as will be discussed in much greater detail in the next chapter, Wheeler would do controversial things in our regions without giving us a heads-up or an opportunity to give any feedback or opinions.

From my limited experience with Administrator Pruitt, that would not have happened. Additionally, based on my interactions with Administrator Pruitt, I think he was a very good man who just made some bad personal decisions that allowed the political vultures in the media to accomplish their ultimate mission of taking him down. That's just where we are as a country at this point.

Anyway, I never had the opportunity to say thank you to Scott Pruitt for giving me the chance to have the best two years of my professional career by serving as the R9 RA for the US EPA. Had you remained the administrator, I am almost certain I would have retained my job until the administration changed, and this book would not have been written. It's been written, however, and it's all thanks to the then new acting administrator, Andrew Wheeler.

The next day, all politicals met at HQ or got on a video or phone from the regions to hear what the new acting administrator had to say. He said it would be business as usual. He said that the agenda had not changed a bit. He said he would look forward to working with all the RAs in the regions on a personal basis—not!—and he said he would be keeping Ryan Jackson on as his COS. He then asked for questions. There was a long pause, and then I unmuted my phone.

"Administrator Wheeler, this is Mike Stoker."

Wheeler responded, "Yes."

"Ken Wagner has been a great asset to me and, I am sure, to all the RAs. Will you be keeping him in the role he had with Administrator Pruitt?"

After a long pause, Wheeler said, "Well, I guess so." (I believe Ken was on the phone from Oklahoma.) "Ken, will you be staying on?"

Ken answered, "Yes, Mr. Administrator. I'd be honored to."

The only thing I cared about from that all-hands was receiving confirmation that the political appointee in HQ whom I respected the most, Ken, would continue on in his role. The call ended shortly after that. Within fifteen minutes, I received a call from Ken thanking me for asking the question. He confirmed to me that no one from HQ had told him one way or another whether he would continue on in his role. I just told Ken I was relieved.

I had been on the job for just sixty days, and he had become the most important and successful conduit, in my opinion, from the regions to HQ, and he did an incredible job in being successful as a conduit. I never felt disconnected from HQ with regard to policy or the agenda when Ken was on the job. When he left to become the secretary of Energy and Environment for the state of Oklahoma, that would change dramatically, at least for me.

I hung up and thought that I was nowhere near as impressed with the one-on-one people skills of Acting Administrator Wheeler as I was with Administrator Pruitt, who had just resigned. Boy, would I soon learn how correct my instincts were. Anyway, week 7 was behind me, and I was looking forward to week 8, which would be a road trip to meet four of my tribes in the Owens Valley.

Week 8

On Monday, the ninth, I arrived at the Southern California Field Office (SCFO) early. My director of the Land, Chemicals and Redevelopment Division, Jeff Scott, and my tribal division director, Laura Ebbert, were flying in from San Francisco. I participated via video in my weekly 10:00 a.m. R9 senior division directors' meeting and my 11:00 a.m. HQ meeting. At noon, the three of us hit the road to visit four tribes in the Owens Valley. My first meeting was with the Lone Pine Tribe. The next day, I would meet with the Fort Independence, Big Pine Paiute, and Bishop Tribes.

While each of the tribes had their own unique issues, one common issue was discussed in each of the tribal visits in the Owens Valley. That issue was the problems associated with the control of the Los Angeles Department of Water and Power (DWP) of the vast majority of water rights in the Owens Valley. If you haven't seen the movie *Chinatown* starring Jack Nicholson, I strongly encourage you to watch it. It is a fictional account of the power of the DWP, their buying up all the water rights in the Owens Valley back in the thirties and forties, and the victims of their water grab.

Driving back to LA later with Scott and Ebbert, I commented to them that I couldn't help but think of the movie after my two days of visits with the four Owens Valley tribes. One thing I promised all four tribes was that I would meet with DWP and strongly encourage them to start a more proactive dialogue with the tribes in the valley, and I promised them that I would make sure that DWP knew that one of the top personal priorities of the new R9 RA was his 148 tribes. Four of those tribes were located in the Owens Valley and had issues with the DWP. DWP would soon find out that if my four tribes in the Owens Valley had issues with the DWP, then the DWP also had issues with me, the new R9 RA.

Before leaving the topic of these four tribes, I need to briefly mention an individual named Alan Bacock. Alan is a member of the Big Pine Paiute Tribe. Alan had been very active in representing the 148 tribes in R9 through his various leadership roles in the R9 Regional Tribal Operations Committee (RTOC). Alan, like every tribal leader I met during my tenure, had a passion for advocating specifically for their individual tribal interests and tribes in general.

Of all the people I met as the R9 RA, Allan was one whom I came to appreciate and respect immensely. I lobbied hard with HQ and, specifically, the Office of International and Tribal Affairs (OITA) that Alan be appointed to an open position that would assure that tribal concerns were heard at HQ. I lobbied as I had already come to believe there was a strong disconnect at the HQ level with the nation's tribes. Alan could change that. Unfortunately, that effort would be unsuccessful.

Three months after my termination, however, I was so happy to hear that R9 hired Alan as the environmental justice coordinator. There is no one who will fight for environmental justice in R9 more than Alan. One last thing about him is, he is not only a passionate advocate for tribal needs. He is also a DJ who hosts an AM radio show in the Owens Valley.

He knows I'm a Deadhead. Scott, Ebbert, and I had dinner with Alan the first night on our visit. Alan said he would dedicate the next day's radio show to the new R9 RA by playing Dead music all day long. When we were driving the next day, he dedicated the song "Truckin'" to me. He couldn't have picked a better Dead song for my dedication. The last couple of lyrics are so much my life and certainly was my life as the R9 RA.

> Sometimes the light's all shinin' on me
> Other times, I can barely see
> Lately, it occurs to me
> What a long, strange trip it's been
> Truckin', I'm going home
> Whoa, Whoa, baby, back where I belong
> Back home, sit down and patch my bones
> And get back truckin' on

My life and what I have done are so much these lyrics. I have always been a fighter for the underdog or the underrepresented. If you knock me down, I'll get back up and come back twice as hard. I suppose this book and my lawsuit against Wheeler et al. are an example of that. There will be more on the lawsuit in the final chapter, "My Termination, the Litigation, and Going Forward."

Anyway, I love the music of the Dead. I especially love the last lyrics of the song "Truckin'," and I came to love my tribes, their tribal members, and their causes. Thank you, Alan, for your dedication. I truly hope our paths professionally cross again someday.

I flew to the San Francisco office on Wednesday morning. The rest of the week would be briefings, briefings, and more briefings.

CHAPTER 4

The First 100 Days (Part 3)

Week 9

WEEK 9 WOULD BE returning to DC to participate in the Executive Leadership Council and the RA/AA national program and regional roundtable. I would also be able to see my good friend Robert O'Brien, who had been sworn in by the secretary of state, Mike Pompeo, as special envoy to the president for hostage affairs in the treaty room of the Department of State. Little did I know that nine months later, John Bolton, the president's national security adviser, would be fired and that Robert would be appointed to replace him. In my opinion, Robert would prove to be the role model of how a national security adviser should serve the nation and the president.

Back to the Executive Leadership Council (ELC). The ELC was an opportunity to bring all the leaders of EPA and tribal leaders together to discuss issues, but more importantly, it was primarily for the leaders of EPA to listen to the tribal leaders' concerns. The meeting only helped solidify the opinion I was starting to develop and would come to firmly believe by my termination that the tribes often got nothing but lip service.

In this case, it was Trump's EPA. However, from everything I saw and became aware of, Trump's EPA gave as much attention to our nation's tribes as past EPA administrations did regardless of party affiliation, nothing more and nothing less. It is a sad commentary, and it is just my personal opinion, but our nation's tribes just don't get the attention and respect they deserve. Again, more on this later.

The ELC was proving to be a huge disappointment. The ELC would be followed by the RA/AA national program and regional roundtable. In this meeting, RAs would be given the opportunity to advocate for certain programs or projects. We would have the opportunity to advocate for the establishment of new national priorities. It wasn't mandatory, but if we believed something should be elevated to the status of a national priority, this was the time to do it. The new RA on the block was about to urge the Trump EPA to establish a new national priority, and the new RA on the block was about to get his butt handed to him and not on a silver platter.

In preparation for this meeting, I worked with my R9 Office of Water director, Tomas Torres, and his staff to compile a briefing paper for the infrastructure needed to address the transboundary sewage problems at the US-Mexico border. R9 and R6, which served Texas, had done substantial work on this issue but had never put together one document identifying all the potential infrastructure projects. What was ultimately compiled was a very rough estimate that the sum of $363 million, with specific projects identified, would be able to substantially eliminate the transboundary sewage problem.

This would include the entire border—from the Gulf of Mexico in Texas where the Rio Grande flowed into the ocean, to the San Diego-Tijuana sector where the Tijuana River flowed into the Pacific Ocean, and to Nogales and Naco in between. For approximately $363 million, the Trump administration could legitimately take credit for the elimination of an ongoing national environmental disaster. I was about to make my presentation.

Our briefing paper and proposal had been provided to HQ the week before to be included in the agenda for everyone to see. Other presentations were made, and then I got up to advocate for my personal priority to eliminate transboundary sewage. I talked about the specific issue and the calamity in the San Diego area. I said this was a national problem.

I mentioned that our initial assessment was that $363 million could essentially get this issue under control, and I underscored that this was a huge opportunity for our administration to respond and deliver on solving a national environmental nightmare that previous administrations refused to address. This could be a huge environmental win. I then sat down, and then Acting Deputy Administrator Henry Darwin spoke.

Darwin went on to say that this was not the fault or responsibility of the EPA. He said the blame was with the International Boundary and Water Commission (IBWC). He asserted that they were the federal entity created by Congress to deal with the problem, and he concluded that IBWC had been derelict in their duties to do just that. As he spoke, you could visibly see how irritated he was by this issue.

His face turned bright red as he spoke. I remember thinking as he spoke that this issue could instantaneously raise his blood pressure by one hundred points, and I wondered why he was so opposed to my idea of the EPA being the heroes in solving this problem. It really didn't matter that the IBWC had been derelict in their efforts, which was an assessment I agreed with. Our EPA and our administration could take credit for the win.

But then it dawned on me. As you may recall, I earlier mentioned that Darwin was the director of the Arizona Department of Environmental Quality prior to Mr. Cabrera becoming the director. Arizona, under Darwin's watch as director of ADEQ, had filed the lawsuit against the IBWC, the same lawsuit that weeks earlier, Ken Wagner, the DOJ, Director Cabrera, and I met in Phoenix to discuss settlement options for.

For Darwin, this was personal. IBWC was the villain. For Darwin, no one was going to bail the IBWC out, especially not the EPA. For me, it really didn't matter who was to be blamed. For me, the mission of the EPA was "to protect human health and the environment." For me, it was taking on an issue that served both our missions, and it would give the Trump administration a huge environmental win.

Unfortunately, under Wheeler's leadership, Trump's EPA would never make addressing transboundary sewage at the US-Mexico border a priority. In fact, as will be addressed later, Wheeler took actions that were intended to get me to back off from pushing this issue. But I am not the kind of person who backs off from something I firmly believe in, and I firmly believed in this issue. I firmly believed pursuing this issue was exactly what the president would want, and I firmly believed our commitment to the EPA's mission required us to address this issue. I wouldn't back off.

On the contrary, I would double down. I would go on to have eight more stakeholder meetings in San Diego. I would work with Mayor Dedina, Mayor Bailey (Coronado), Mayor Faulconer (San Diego), San Diego supervisor Greg Cox, representatives of the US Customs and Border Protection, retired members of the US Navy, San Diego's port authority, the congressional offices of Congressman Juan Vargas and Scott Peters, and other interested parties. I would give them the briefing paper I provided HQ showing the $363 million project costs with specific infrastructure projects identified.

Giving members of the public this briefing paper was perfectly ethical. It was not a confidential working document but a fact sheet that any interested member of the public was entitled to. I would tell those stakeholders that while I could not ethically advocate for anything with Congress, they could. I would be a conduit to them for whatever information they needed. I would provide them the information they needed. They would be the advocates with Congress that I wasn't ethically allowed to be.

In the end, Darwin's efforts that day at HQ in DC failed. However, Speaker Pelosi's COS, Robert Edmonson, called me mid-December 2019. He told me that the speaker of the house, in the final negotiations with the White House over agreeing to the US-Mexico trade agreement, said that they had a deal if the White House added a $350 million appropriation to the US EPA to address transboundary sewage at the US-Mexico border for the San Diego-Tijuana sector. The White House agreed, and EPA now had $350 million to finally address this issue.

Yes, Henry, the IBWC had been derelict in their approach to this problem and in their commitment in trying to solve this problem. But no, Henry, the answer was not to let the problem continue and point the finger at the IBWC. This was a great opportunity for our EPA, for Trump's EPA, and that day in July, the EPA squandered that opportunity. Thanks to the stakeholders in San Diego, President Trump, and Speaker Pelosi, the issue will now finally be addressed, at least for the San Diego-Tijuana sector.

As previously stated, Ken Wagner started the advocacy, and I picked up the baton and ran with it. The assistant administrator for the Office of Water, David Ross, had also been a strong advocate. I always thought he, too, believed it should have been an EPA national priority, but he was an HQ guy and had to work in HQ day in and day out with those who didn't want it to be a priority. He had to work with Henry Darwin. So from his perspective, if the others didn't want it to be a priority, he had plenty of other issues to focus on. I didn't have to work in HQ, and I would continue to give 100 percent to make sure this issue would be addressed, and it was finally addressed thanks to the San Diego stakeholders, Speaker Pelosi, and President Trump.

Week 10

Week 10 would put me in Northern California to meet with one more of my R9 tribes, the Hoopa Valley Tribe. I would also visit one of the largest Superfund projects in the nation, the Iron Mountain Mine Superfund site. I would end my week with meetings in Sacramento.

On Monday morning, I caught an early morning flight from LAX to Arcata. I was met at the airport by my tribes division director, Laura Ebbert. We departed in a rental car for a two-hour drive up to the Hoopa tribal lands. There, I was joined by Dana Barton, a Superfund project manager and an R9 geologist. I then met with the tribal council, after which we toured an area above the Trinity River. The Hoopa Valley Tribe had been advocating for the Copper Bluff

Mine to be added to the National Priorities List (NPL) of Superfund sites.

The mines were located a thousand feet above the Trinity River on very steep slopes that drained directly down into the river. From the mine openings, you could see dirty, rustic colors of red and brown that followed the slope from the opening in the mines all the way down to the river. Everything you looked at was beautiful, except for the mine opening and the slopes directly below them.

R9 had done extensive geological studies of the Copper Bluff Mine. We established that tribal and nontribal fishermen were being exposed to the acid mine drainage while engaging in fishing activities near the site. Our staff and the Hoopa Valley Tribe were also concerned that the metals leaking into the Trinity River had a negative impact on aquatic species, including lampreys and green sturgeon, which are traditional subsistence foods of the Hoopa people.

From the staff briefings prior to my visit, I had already decided I would be advocating that the Copper Bluff Mine be added to the NPL. I advised the tribal council of my decision in my meeting. They were relieved and appreciative. On May 13, 2019, I was happy to report to the tribe that the mine had officially been added to the Superfund NPL. In the press release HQ issued that day announcing the decision, I was quoted saying, "The Hoopa Valley Tribe and the tribal fishery are still affected by this mine, despite its closure decades ago. Adding the site to the National Priorities List is an important step towards cleaning up this toxic legacy."

When the tour ended, we left to drive across the Klamath Mountains to Redding. There, we would stay overnight. We would then depart the next morning for a tour of the largest Superfund site in the US: Iron Mountain. Before leaving the story of the Copper Bluff Mine, however, I want to mention one more thing that came out of the tour other than listing the mine on the NPL.

During the tour, one of our geologists mentioned how difficult it was to do the assessment since the EPA was prohibited from using drones. I asked, "What? We're the EPA, and we are not allowed to use drones? What are you talking about?" He proceeded to tell me that at some time in the past, the EPA was using a drone, and it ended up being used in an enforcement action. The use of a drone for enforcement actions became very controversial, and the EPA administrator at the time issued a blanket prohibition against the use of drones by the agency for any reason.

I've been a probusiness, antiregulatory attorney and politician. If anyone would be against using drones for enforcement actions, it would be me. To prohibit the use of drones, however, for doing things like site assessments for Superfund purposes or to assist in federally declared emergencies just made no sense to me at all.

When the week was over, I started advocating with HQ for the use of drones in limited circumstances, like Superfund site assessments and federally declared disasters. In December, as my R9 emergency management staff was responding to Super Typhoon Yutu and the Camp and Woolsey Fires, Administrator Wheeler agreed to my request and issued a directive that the use of drones in federally declared disasters was acceptable under certain conditions that the RA would attest to. In January 2019, EPA drones flew again for the first time in many years in doing site assessments of the damage from Super Typhoon Yutu on Tinian.

Back to Iron Mountain. The drive from the Hoopa Valley Tribe to Redding took several hours more than we had planned, as a fire had broken out in the Klamath Mountains, and the direct route had been closed. After six hours, we arrived in Redding. The next morning, Dana Barton and I were met by my Superfund and emergency management director, Enrique Manzanilla, and his deputy, John Lyons. We departed for Iron Mountain.

While the name Iron Mountain may sound like a Disneyland ride, the real Iron Mountain is the story of an environmental disaster that has become a huge EPA Superfund success story. Iron Mountain Mine was mined for iron, silver, gold, copper, zinc, and pyrite intermittently from the 1860s until 1963.

The mine is the source of extremely acidic mine drainage that also contains large amounts of zinc, copper, and cadmium. The drainage water from the Iron Mountain Mine is the most acidic water naturally found on earth. Some samples collected in 1990 and 1991 have been measured to have a pH of -3.6. About seventy thousand people use surface water within three miles of the mine as their source of water.

The mine was designated as a Superfund site in 1983. In 2000, the government reached a settlement with the Aventis CropScience, now part of Bayer, for long-term funding of the cleanup efforts. From what I recall, the amount of money in the trust fund is almost $1 billion. Mitigation of the site involves the installation and operation of a full-scale neutralization system, a fully operable landfill only for Iron Mountain processed materials, the capping of the areas of the mine, and the construction and operation of the Slickrock Creek Retention Reservoir to collect contaminated runoff for treatment.

From this operation, the diversion of the Upper Spring Creek into the neutralization system greatly increased the ability of the EPA and the Bureau of Reclamation to manage the continuing release of contaminants from the site to minimize harm to the Sacramento River ecosystem. At one time, the site literally dumped five thousand acre-feet of water a day of polluted waters into the Sacramento River. Today, virtually nothing.

While many think of regulations and enforcement when they hear about the EPA, from my years as RA, I think of things like the incredible work the R9 Superfund staff has done in places like Iron Mountain. I'll get into many more examples of this in the chapter "Superfund and Emergency Management."

We concluded the tour, and I headed with Enrique to Sacramento. My COS, Amy Miller, would meet us there. I addressed a joint meeting of the California Business Roundtable and the California Independent Petroleum Association in Sacramento, and we then departed for San Francisco.

That Wednesday, I had several briefings with staff regarding several upcoming issues. I also had a meeting with Sandy Fabritz, the governmental relations director with Freeport-McMoRan (FM). FM is one of the largest mining operations in the US and the largest copper producer of any public company in the world. FM operates seven open-pit copper mines (Morenci, Baghdad, Safford, Sierrita, and Miami) in Arizona located within R9 and Chino and Tyrone in New Mexico. It also operates two molybdenum mines (Henderson and Climax) in Colorado. The meeting was intended as an introduction. I will say, FM is lucky to have Sandy. Sandy made it very clear that if I ever had questions or concerns, I should feel free to call her 24-7. I extended the same offer to her as our meeting ended.

A couple more briefings followed, then we were off to the San Francisco office to fly to LAX for a day in the SCFO on Thursday. I had several meetings and video briefings and left at 7:00 p.m. to drive home to Carpinteria. On Friday, I would telework from home as week 10 came to a close.

Week 11

I started the week of July 30 in the SCFO. Monday would be another day in the world of Superfund. At 9:00 a.m., I had a staff briefing about the Orange County North Basin. I had been advised by staff in earlier briefings that their recommendation would be to add the basin as the next R9 Superfund NPL site.

That basin focuses on a six-and-a-half-square-mile portion of the groundwater aquifer located under Fullerton, Anaheim, and Placentia. Manufacturing industries operating primarily in the 1950s, 1960s, and 1970s left a legacy of industrial pollutants at the former factories. The pollutants—mostly volatile organic compounds (VOCs), including solvents and degreasers—have migrated through the soils and are now leaching into the underlying groundwater basin. The companies involved are major players in the Southern California region. They include Northrop Grumman Corp., Alcoa Corp., and Chicago Musical Instruments, among others.

The Orange County Water District had been trying for years to work with all the responsible parties to provide an adequate response. Many companies had entered into settlement agreements with the district for funding remediation efforts. At the time I was sworn in, several of the larger players were holdouts. The district had lost all patience and believed the Superfund NPL listing was the only option remaining to obtain the funding from all those responsible to fully remediate. The price tag for remediation will most likely cost hundreds of millions of dollars. Once added to the NPL, the EPA will go after all responsible parties to fund their share of the Superfund remediation efforts.

I met with the attorneys and the CEOs for most of the companies opposing the Superfund listing. I also met with the Orange County Water District board and its executive director. I came up with an alternative, too, of which very few people involved with Superfund issues are even aware.

On the morning of the thirtieth, I told my staff that I wanted to pursue an alternative to a listing agreement (ALA) with all the responsible parties. Most of the companies assured me they would be supportive. What an ALA would accomplish was, it would create a binding agreement under which the EPA would have as much authority as it would with a Superfund listing while allowing the parties to avoid the stigma and other consequences of a formal listing. The agreement would provide the course of action going forward, and all the responsible parties would be bound and signatory to the agreement.

I told the companies that I fully supported listing the basin on the EPA Superfund NPL. I also told them that if we could finalize an ALA agreement by October 2018, I would not pursue a formal listing. They were not happy about the only option I left them, but they knew they had run out of options. It would be an ALA or an NPL listing.

The Orange County Water District did not oppose my direction. They made it very clear that after ten years of many of these companies giving them the runaround, they were very skeptical that they would ultimately agree. I told them they could very well be right but wanted to give them the one last opportunity to pursue the ALA. The district now knew that one way or another, they would get what they needed. It would either be by an ALA or an NPL listing. It is important to note that the EPA always retains the right to add the site to the NPL even if an ALA is entered into as an initial option.

Our meeting ended. They had their marching orders to advise the parties of the ALA option. After six months, just as the district had predicted, a couple of the major players who had told me they would support an ALA ultimately decided not to. I then advised my staff to proceed to list the water basin on the EPA Superfund NPL. I gave it my best. I tried something new and was disappointed that those who assured me they would agree to an ALA failed to do so. The district was right. I was wrong. I put it down in the category of Nothing Ventured, Nothing gained. As for the outcome, in September 2020, seven months after I was terminated, the Orange County North Basin was added to the EPA Superfund NPL.

After the Orange County North Basin meeting with my staff finished, I participated by video in my 10:00 a.m. senior staff meeting and 11:00 a.m. HQ staff meeting. After the meeting, Dana Barton, who had accompanied me on the Copper Bluff Mine and Iron Mountain tour, and a couple other R9 Superfund staff met me in the Los Angeles Field Office. We then left for Hawthorne to tour the Montrose Superfund site and to meet with concerned citizens who lived in the area surrounding Montrose.

Dana joined me, as she was the Montrose Superfund project manager. Dana, like all the rest of her R9 colleagues, is an incredibly dedicated EPA staffer. What she does, she does very well. I immediately came to respect her for the job she was doing. Being a project manager is a very difficult task. You are generally dealing with a very controversial topic around which the public, understandably, has major concerns. You need to address the problem, but you also have to gain the public's trust and convince them that the EPA is indeed protecting their health and their environment. That is a huge challenge that Dana and her fellow project managers do so well.

My staff and I met for lunch with the concerned citizens. I gave them the story of my past as a county supervisor advocating for the NPL listing of Casmalia, underscoring that my then constituents were given the protections they deserved. I assured them that as their R9 RA, I wanted to provide them the same assurances in regard to Montrose.

Then it was off to tour the Superfund site. The thirteen-acre Montrose Chemical Co. site was the location of a dichlorodiphenyltrichloroethane (DDT) manufacturing facility from 1947 to 1982. Between the late 1950s and the early 1970s, the company was responsible for the discharging of an estimated 1,700 tons of DDT into the ocean via the county's sewer system. In addition, the company dumped hundreds of thousands of barrels containing waste laced with DDT at a deep-sea site located between the California coast and Catalina Island.

Needless to say, the dumping of these toxic wastes created a marine biology disaster. The impact on local fish was tremendous, requiring numerous fish consumption advisories and health warnings. Bald eagles on Catalina, as recently as 2007, were unable to reproduce because the DDT had caused their eggshells to become too thin.

In October 1989, Montrose was added to the Superfund NPL. In 1990, the US and California filed lawsuits against Montrose and nine other facilities near the Palos Verdes Peninsula, citing damages to the nearby marine environment. In December 2000, Montrose and three other corporations settled their lawsuit for a collective $73 million, bringing the total up to $140 million to fund the restoration of the Palos Verdes Shelf marine environment.

In addition to the restoration of the Palos Verdes Shelf marine environment, the Superfund NPL included remediation to the water basin that had been polluted by Montrose's operations, specifically the Montrose / Del Amo dual site groundwater basin, which had been polluted with chlorobenzene, benzene, and various chlorinated solvents.

Like many of the Superfund sites located in Southern California involving pollution of the water basin (a list that includes San Fernando Valley and San Gabriel Valley), incredible water treatment operations have been put in place to continue to extract the toxins out of the water basins. Ideally, over time, this will restore the basins to safe, natural levels, eliminating the need for these treatment facilities. That day is still many decades away. Once a mine or a water basin is listed on the NPL, it is not unreasonable to expect it to remain there for many, many, many decades.

The tour ended, and my staff departed for the airport to fly back to San Francisco. I headed back to the SCFO to review documents and staff reports and then headed to LAX. I would spend over to

LAX to fly to San Francisco, to attend to matters in the San Francisco office and then fly back to Orange County for a Wednesday morning meeting. I would then drive up to Morro Bay on Wednesday for a tour of the Morro Bay estuary the next day. This would be a special day, as Morro Bay was in my neck of the woods. I had hiked the area numerous times in my life, but I never thought I would be hiking it someday as the R9 RA.

The next morning, I arrived at the Morro Bay National Estuary Program office to meet Executive Director Lexie Bell and her staff. I spent the day touring the estuary and also met for lunch with the mayor of Morro Bay. The city of Morro Bay was going for a Water Infrastructure Finance and Innovation Act (WIFIA) grant. I let the mayor know I would be in full support of their request at HQ but reminded them it was HQ that scored the projects and ultimately decided who would get WIFIA funding. I was very happy to hear that a couple of months after I left the EPA, the city of Morro Bay was awarded that WIFIA grant.

The estuary is located between Santa Barbara and Monterey. The following is according to the EPA website:

> The 2,300-acre estuary is home to a working, fishing fleet and recreational boaters. Morro Bay provides important habitat for birds, fish, and other animals. It is a vital stop for migrating birds on the Pacific Flyway… The Morro Bay Estuary Program is one of 28 estuaries nationwide designated and funded by the US EPA as National Estuary Projects (NEP) due to their national significance.
>
> The Morro Bay NEP protects and restores the important estuarine and watershed resources through on the ground projects, partnerships, and education. The Morro Bay NEP and its partners monitor water and sediment quality, habitat and species.

The Morro Bay NEP is truly an environmental gem. If you are ever visiting San Luis Obispo, I strongly encourage you to visit it. If you run into the executive director of the program, Ms. Lexie Bell, tell her I said hi and thank her for the good work she is doing.

Weeks 12 and 13

I would fly to Honolulu on Tuesday, August 7. I would spend two days there for meetings with Admiral Fort and a tour of Red Hill, as well as a meeting with Honolulu mayor Kirk Caldwell to discuss stormwater runoff issues involving the city of Honolulu and to tour the Hawaii Institute of Marine Biology and the Gates Coral Lab.

On Wednesday morning, I arrived at Naval Station Pearl Harbor. My COS and I were escorted into Admiral Fort's office. Our topic? The Red Hill Underground Fuel Storage tanks. The Red Hill Underground Fuel Storage Facility is a military fuel storage facility that serves Pearl Harbor's and many of the Pacific Fleet's fuel demands.

Unlike any other facility in the United States, Red Hill can store up to 250 million gallons of fuel. It consists of twenty steel-lined, underground storage tanks encased in concrete and built into the cavities that were mined inside Red Hill. Each tank has a storage capacity of approximately 12.5 million gallons.

Before the US entered World War II, the Roosevelt administration became concerned about the vulnerability of the many aboveground fuel storage tanks at Pearl Harbor. In 1940, the Roosevelt administration decided to build Red Hill. In December 2013, contractors completed a three-year scheduled routine maintenance upgrade on Tank 5 at Red Hill. At the conclusion of the overhaul in January 2014, the navy initiated a return to service evolution, refilling the tank with jet fuel (JP-8).

During this process, the inventory management alarms sounded. As a result of faulty work and poor-quality welds, 27,000 gallons of jet fuel was spilled. The state of Hawaii and EPA's initial concern was whether the spill reached the groundwater. To date, all test results for contamination of the drinking water have come back well within safe drinking water standards. The spill, however, drove some concerned citizens to try to close down Red Hill.

The EPA's role has been to assure that the navy strictly abides by the timetable agreed to in a consent decree (CD) entered into several years ago. There are eight sections in the CD. One of the key sections that is most relevant today is the seventh: "Development of future groundwater protection and evaluation."

Pursuant to section 7, R9 staff have been working with the navy to find a pathway forward. That pathway could include dismantling all of Red Hill and building fuel tanks elsewhere or establishing protocols going forward that define how the existing tanks will be protected and maintained to assure no future spills.

In November 2019, the Sierra Club of Hawaii filed a lawsuit against the Hawaii State Department of Health. The Sierra Club challenged the department's proposed rule amendments allowing underground storage tank permit applications, including Red Hill, to be automatically approved after 180 days. In referencing the lawsuit, the Sierra Club of Hawaii stated, "This lawsuit was about making sure the Health Department actually does its job to protect the health of Hawaii's people and environment. It's outrageous that the department would be willing to approve the operation of Red Hill tanks knowing the extreme risk they pose to Oahu's water supply."

As it stands today, the EPA will continue to interface with the navy with ongoing risk and vulnerability assessment studies. Back when I met Admiral Fort, there was a great deal more uncertainty. What would the future provide? I was meeting with the admiral to discuss that path forward. Our meeting was followed by a tour inside Red Hill. It was an engineering marvel.

Inside the mountain, we went on top of one of the tanks that was empty and undergoing routine maintenance. On the walkway to the center of the tank, looking down into an abyss, the admiral stated that this location always reminded him of the scene in *Star Wars* where there was a lightsaber fight on a walkway with nothing but an empty abyss below. I couldn't agree more. I dropped a penny.

It seemed to fall for at least ten seconds into darkness before you could hear the faint sound of it hitting the floor below.

We returned from the tour, and I thanked Admiral Fort for the time he had taken to give me the tour of Red Hill. I underscored that R9 wanted to work closely with the navy but that it was going to be really important to do that much more working with the local stakeholders so the public's confidence in the navy could be restored. In a lot of ways, Red Hill was, to the people of Honolulu, what Hunters Point Superfund site was to the people of San Francisco. Both involved the navy, and in both cases, the local public had lost their trust or confidence as a result of how the navy had handled the situation.

Indeed, Red Hill had become to Hawaii congresswoman Tulsi Gabbard and Congressman Ed Case what Hunters Point had become to Speaker Pelosi; and to them, I gave my personal assurances that the EPA was going to be transparent going forward regarding Red Hill and Hunters Point respectively. Congresswoman Gabbard and Congressman Case, like Speaker Pelosi regarding Hunters Point, had expressed to me in earlier meetings how appreciative they were for the approach I was taking with regard to Red Hill.

The next day, I met with Mayor Caldwell, and we discussed the need for Honolulu to do more in addressing the city of Honolulu's stormwater drainage problems. I underscored the potential availability of millions of WIFIA dollars and that R9 was there to assist wherever we could. I also underscored, however, that this was a serious, ongoing issue that needed to be addressed.

When heavy downpours occur, the Honolulu stormwater drainage system is just not designed to retain the waters that become polluted from flowing over streets, the sewer, etc. As a result, these waters end up in and around the Pacific Ocean at and near Waikiki. I am not going to get into the details, but let's just leave it at this.

As much as I have come to respect Mayor Caldwell and though I know he is doing as much as he can with the resources he's been given to address stormwater discharge into the ocean, I will never swim at Waikiki within seventy-two hours of a major Honolulu rain event, and I am an ocean swimmer who loves starting or ending the day with an ocean swim, something I did many times while in Honolulu, including on the day I met with the mayor. Hopefully, more progress has been made on this issue since my termination. This is an issue the city of Honolulu, the state of Hawaii, and the US EPA need to do more on to fully address and to provide the public with the protection they deserve from stormwater runoff in the city of Honolulu.

I will discuss this issue in much greater detail later in the book. However, suffice it to say that in many of our major US cities, the wastewater infrastructure is just not adequate to process stormwater discharge. This is especially a problem in our major coastal cities, where the overflow ultimately ends up in the nearby ocean. In the chapter "Policy Recommendations for EPA Going Forward," I strongly recommend that Congress include substantial appropriations in any future infrastructure legislation to address these wastewater infrastructure needs to respond to stormwater discharges.

On Thursday morning, I toured the Hawaii Institute of Marine Biology. This institute is doing great work, especially in the area of coral reef resiliency. Many of our world's coral reefs are dying off and being bleached out by what many marine biologists believe is being caused by warmer ocean temperatures. There are, however, some super coral reefs that, for whatever reason, have thrived in warmer waters.

As a member representing the EPA on the US Coral Reef Task Force, which would take me to American Samoa the following week for the annual meeting, I spent more time dealing with the issue of coral reefs and their protection and enhancement than any other political appointee in Trump's EPA. Like so many aspects of my job, this was just one more reason why I often stated and truly believed that I had the best job in America as the R9 RA. I also said, rather prophetically, that when my job was ever a disappointment, it would inevitably always have something to do with HQ and something I had no control over.

After touring the institute, it was off to the airport to catch a flight to spend week 13 in American Samoa. Many of the attendees for the Coral Reef Task Force (CRTF) meeting were on my flight.

I also had my Pacific Islands director, John McCarroll, with me. In addition to participating in the CRTF meeting, I would be in American Samoa for the week to deal with American Samoa EPA issues, along with John and R9's Pacific Islands Division senior engineer, Carl Goldstein.

Upon arriving around 9:00 p.m., we were met on the tarmac by airport security and the director of the American Samoa EPA, Ameko Pato. We embraced each other with a bear hug. I had met Ameko in San Francisco two months earlier during the R9 Pacific Islands conference. In American Samoa, the R9 RA was considered a VIP. Accordingly, they then took me through a side gate into the Governor's Lounge. I was asked if I wanted anything to drink and if I would give them my passport. I grabbed a bottle of water.

Ameko and I talked. He said he was really looking forward to Sunday, when we would see each other again at a barbecue American Samoa EPA was hosting for the US EPA staff. He told me how special my trip the next day would be. Some of the members of the CRTF and I would be going to Manu'a Islands and Faleasi'u for an opportunity to tour some incredible coral reefs. I would return to Pago Pago International Airport on Saturday, early afternoon.

After this exchange, someone returned with my passport stamped, and the director escorted me outside, where three American Samoan EPA Cadillac Escalades with police-type lights on their roofs were flashing red. I was escorted into the second Escalade, and we departed with sirens turned on toward Sadie's by the Sea. I told my driver there really was no need for the lights or the sirens, but he insisted.

No more than ten minutes had elapsed from the time I stepped down on the tarmac to departing in the Escalade to Sadie's by the Sea. For everyone else, it took approximately one hour. When I called my wife to give her a recap of my VIP treatment in American Samoa, she reminded me that when she picked me up at LAX on my return, I would not be escorted into a Governor's Lounge, there would be no lights flashing on our Kia Optima, and I certainly would no longer be a VIP. She left me with, "Enjoy it while you are there."

As promised, the trip to Manu'a Islands and Faleasi'u was beyond amazing. Back in American Samoa, my staff and I met that afternoon for briefings on the upcoming week. Following the briefings, John and I went for a late-afternoon snorkeling in the coral reefs in the bay in front of Sadie's by the Sea, where we were staying. John and I would probably have over thirty more snorkeling trips like this before I left the EPA.

My staff always presented me with completely thorough briefings. The next day, however, would bring something that was impossible to brief and impossible to anticipate. The next day would be a real challenge, testing my ability to adapt to totally unforeseeable circumstances. It would also become a test for the American Samoa EPA.

The next day, John, Carl, and I had breakfast, went back to our rooms to go over emails, and agreed we would meet at noon to drive out to where the American Samoa EPA was hosting a barbecue. We met at noon and drove out to the barbecue. Once there, I was greeted by Ameko. Again, we gave each other a traditional American Samoa bear hug. I also gave bear hugs to the other American Samoan EPA staff whom I had met on Thursday night at the airport. We were all socializing with one another.

Approximately an hour after I arrived, Director Pato and I both addressed the attendees. I reminded them what I had told all in attendance at the Pacific Islands conference in San Francisco two months earlier—that all the Pacific Island territories would be one of my top personal priorities as RA. I was so honored to be in American Samoa and was looking forward to spending the week touring numerous American Samoa EPA and R9 EPA joint projects, I said.

I underscored how much R9 appreciated the incredible work Ameko had been doing and how he had done an amazing job in turning the American Samoa EPA around since becoming director several years earlier. What had once been a so-so relationship between the two agencies had become a very close, positive relationship. That was all as a result of Ameko. He really left an incredible legacy. (More on that later.)

We then all sat down and ate traditional American Samoan foods. Calling this meal beyond delicious would be an understatement. And then it happened. Ameko was sitting on a chair, having difficulty breathing. His staff was putting wet towels on his neck and waving towels in front of his face to cool him off. I told his staff they needed to get him to the hospital. Ameko didn't want to go, but finally, his wife and staff would not take no for an answer. They put him in the back of a truck, and off to the hospital they went.

Several hours later, John, Carl, and I went to a restaurant-bar to meet up with several of the CRTF attendees. It was then that John got the call. Ameko had passed away. This had to be one of the most surreal moments in my life. John, Carl, and I discussed what to do. I said we should go to the hospital to pay our respects to Ameko's family. John agreed, and we left for the hospital, stopping at Sadie's only for a change of clothes.

We arrived at the hospital. Pursuant to American Samoan tradition, Ameko's body had already been put in an open casket in the hospital chapel. Also pursuant to tradition, there would be a funeral ceremony to honor Ameko. As a result of the humidity in American Samoa, it is quite common to have an open casket ceremony at the hospital upon death. This is because a body decomposes quicker under these humid conditions.

In the hospital chapel, the governor, the American Samoan EPA staff, and Ameko's family and friends had all gathered. John and I arrived and gave our personal condolences to Ameko's wife and family and his EPA staff. We reached out to Ameko's deputy, Fa'amao Asalele, who would become a true personal friend in the months to come. Fa'amao, that night, would be named acting director of the American Samoa EPA by the governor.

The intention had been that Ameko and I would meet the next day with Governor Lolo Matalasi Moliga to discuss what was to become a huge issue and challenge for me: the consent decree involving StarKist and the US EPA that was in place for Clean Water Act violations. StarKist was the largest employer in American Samoa, and the governor wanted relief from the consent decree, as StarKist was threatening to close down the one remaining cannery if concessions were not made. A second cannery had already been closed down. The next morning, it would be Fa'amao, not Ameko, who would be accompanying me to my meeting with the governor to discuss StarKist and the consent decree.

A minister or priest came in, and we had a short funeral proceeding. We paid our respects and said our goodbyes. Fa'amao, John, and I discussed the next morning. I would meet them at the American Samoa EPA office, and we would walk across the parking lot to the government building to meet with the governor. I gave Fa'amao a big bear hug as we left.

The next morning, John and I arrived at the American Samoa EPA building. Fa'amao had been delayed by phone conversations with the governor. When he arrived, we walked over to the government building. We went up to the governor's office and were ushered into his conference room. While I had anticipated a meeting just between our team, the governor, and Fa'amao, ten minutes later, the entire cabinet of the governor arrived and sat down at the table.

Everyone introduced themselves. The one person who stood out was the attorney general, Talauega E. V. Ale, who is now American Samoa's lieutenant governor. With the exception of Attorney General Ale, every member of the cabinet was wearing slacks and a casual, button-up, collared American Samoa shirt. Talauega, in contrast, was wearing what appeared to be a very expensive Armani suit. For American Samoa, Hawaii, or any of the Pacific Island territories, this was way overdressed. My first impression, in a positive way, was that this was a man who very seldom failed in accomplishing what he wanted.

When the time came for me to speak, I gave the governor my three-minute, canned "I love the Pacific Island territories" speech. I also mentioned how much of a loss it was losing Ameko and what he had accomplished as the American Samoa EPA director. The governor then went straight into StarKist.

StarKist entered a consent decree (CD) with the EPA years earlier for Clean Water Act violations. As a result of that order, one of the two StarKist canneries had closed. The governor asserted that he needed my support to change the CD, or the last cannery would close down as well. He said that he was creating a task force to deal with the issue and that AG Salo Ale would be its chairman. They would be making recommendations to R9 regarding the CD.

I told the governor that I understood where he was coming from, and I assured him that I would do whatever I could but that the Clean Water Act needed to be complied with. The same bay that John and I snorkeled in two days earlier had been dying until the EPA entered into a consent decree several years earlier. As a result, the coral reef had been revived, and the bay, which was a place where locals wouldn't even swim in years earlier, was now clean and full of recreational life. I wasn't going to support any course of action that would reverse these positive developments.

When the governor mentioned the task force, I made it clear that the best way to help American Samoa accomplish some relief for StarKist with regard to the CD was to let the American Samoa EPA be the lead at the table in advocating for what American Samoa wanted. I said Fa'amao and his colleagues at the American Samoa EPA knew what could and what couldn't be done. I then asked the governor, "I assume Fa'amao is on your task force?" There was at least a two- to three-second delay, and then the governor said, "Of course."

The governor looked at the task force as an entity advocating for jobs and the economy. I knew that everyone else on the task force would only be concerned about jobs and how important it was for the American Samoan economy to keep StarKist open. I also knew, however, that the only way a consent decree would be amended with the necessary approval of the EPA and DOJ would be if Fa'amao could assure that all the other task force members understood the EPA restraints. He knew what was reasonable to ask for and what wasn't.

The governor allowed Fa'amao and his staff to assume the role I had advocated for. As a result, in March of 2020, the consent decree was modified. It would help preserve jobs and the environment, which the governor wanted, while at the same time assure that the Clean Water Act was complied with as it related to the StarKist canneries in American Samoa, which was what I wanted.

At the end of the day, it was a true success story for both the economy and the environment. It underscored a philosophy I have maintained over the years in the various public servant positions in which I have served: You don't have to be against the economy to be for the environment, and you don't have to be against the environment to be for the economy. You can be for both.

That week was somewhat contentious with regard to my dealings with the governor. I think he wanted the new kid on the block who was now RA of R9 to just fold when it came to jobs. That was a position I had taken many times in my life, so I understood it and respected it, but I was now responsible for assuring that the environmental laws the EPA enforced were complied with. That meant I had to be firm in saying that American Samoa's pathway to success required the governor allowing American Samoa EPA to steer their task force in the right direction. That was what happened, and that was why a win-win was realized in March 2020 with the modified consent decree.

The crazy circumstances of that week left me and Fa'amao very close friends. It was tough for us to lose Ameko, and it was tough for Fa'amao to assume the position of acting director under these circumstances. We all did what we had to do that week, however. The most important message I sent was to underscore to the governor that Fa'amao was my man when it came to the StarKist consent decree. I made it clear to all that when it came to anything involving EPA and American Samoa, they should go through Fa'amao. They did, and everyone got what they wanted.

As for the governor, I think the world of him. I have the greatest respect for Governor Lolo Moliga. He did exactly what I would have done if I were the governor of American Samoa. It was his job to advocate for the economy and for StarKist. It was my job to advocate for the environment and make sure our environmental laws were enforced.

In looking back and reflecting, I have to say that I was incredibly impressed with the person the governor would introduce as the chairman of the StarKist task force, the then attorney general and now lieutenant governor of American Samoa. Someday, as I predicted to John while in American Samoa, I believe he will be governor, and the people of American Samoa will be lucky to have him in that position. Lieutenant Governor Va'alele did an exemplary job in representing American Samoa on the task force, and Fa'amao did an exemplary job in being the facilitator between what the governor wanted and what R9 could do.

Word had gotten out to most of the attendees of the CRTF about what the governor had asked me to do and how I had responded. This was not only a test of how the rookie RA would respond to pressure from a governor but also a test of my commitment to clean and healthy oceans and the protection of our coral reefs.

In the reception and dinner later in the conference, the then lieutenant governor, now governor, Lemanu Palepoi Mauga was the keynote speaker. Keep in mind that this was an audience that cared about one thing: protecting our oceans and coral reefs. For the majority in this audience, there was no contest between jobs and the coral reefs. Our restaurant was right on the bay that had benefited from the EPA's CD mandating the corrective/remediation efforts by StarKist. The CD had worked. The bay was clean and was coming back to life, along with its coral reefs. For Lieutenant Governor Mauga, towing that line with this audience was a bold move, and he immediately gained huge respect in my mind.

Anyone in politics knows that you try to focus on what you have in common with your audience when you are giving a keynote speech. This audience wanted to hear about cleaner oceans and restored coral reefs, but StarKist was huge for American Samoa and their jobs.

At that time, I really thought StarKist played their cards perfectly with the government of American Samoa. StarKist successfully left American Samoa believing that if they didn't get the relief they needed, they would close down the last remaining cannery. That would have been a devastating blow to the job market in American Samoa.

As a result, the governor told me in our Monday morning meeting what the lieutenant governor would repeat at our dinner/reception keynote speech: "If American Samoa has to pick between jobs or the environment, we will pick jobs." To the CRTF audience, that message took a lot of guts and courage. Lieutenant Governor Mauga had both.

And then the unexpected happened. The MC introduced me and asked if I would give some closing comments for the group. I looked at John with that "What do I do now?" look on my face. He looked back with the same look. This was totally impromptu. I had prepared nothing, as neither myself nor my staff thought I would be asked to provide comments.

I got up and went to the podium. I thanked Lieutenant Governor Mauga and American Samoa for hosting the CRTF annual meeting. I then went on to ask everyone to look at the bay just outside the outdoor dining area where we were sitting. I pointed out that not so many years ago, the bay had been dying. The coral reef had been bleaching out. Today, as a result of the CD with StarKist and a wastewater treatment facility the EPA had helped fund, I said the bay had come back to life. Locals again swam in the beach. The coral reef was coming back faster than anyone anticipated.

I said that I appreciated Lieutenant Governor Mauga's comments but that it didn't have to be about either the environment or the economy and jobs. I promised I would work hard to find a place where the CD could be modified to keep the StarKist cannery open without compromising the environment or the aquatic health of this bay. I also made it very clear, however, that I would not compromise in any way. That meant a reversal of the progress we all had made. If I had to pick between jobs or the environment, then I was duty bound, in this case, to pick the environment.

In my final comments, I suggested that American Samoa look at the tourist/recreational value of promoting their clean oceans, coral reefs, and aquatic treasures. That could mean substantial jobs to boost the economy as well. I still believe that aspect has not been pursued to the level it could that would generate huge annual revenues for the government of American Samoa.

I finished my comments, and I returned to my table. John looked at me and said, "Wow. You just hit it out of the park. Great job!" The event ended, and I went up to the lieutenant governor and again personally thanked him. I told him I respected the position he and the governor had to take, and I stated that I hoped he understood the position I had to take as well. I again underscored, too, that Fa'amao and the American Samoa EPA could help us both get to where we wanted. I ended that evening and returned to my motel room thinking how impressed I was with the lieutenant governor and his willingness to stand firm in the lion's den.

The rest of the week was attending events put on by the CRTF and touring joint projects of the R9 EPA and American Samoa EPA. Over the week, I came to know and became very close with Fa'amao and all his staff. On Wednesday, I provided opening comments to the CRTF annual meeting. I talk about how this week, the environment lost a legend. We lost Ameko Pato.

I asked for a moment of silence and then reminded them that Ameko had taken an American Samoa EPA with just over 10 percent of their employees having higher than a high school diploma to 100 percent having a college degree. I believe over 30 percent of the current staff have a master's or higher.

My R9 staff had told me how problematic it was dealing with American Samoa EPA before Ameko. After Ameko, it was a great, close working relationship. I concluded with my commitment to Ameko that part of his legacy would be my promise to protect his ocean, his bays, and his coral reef. RIP, my friend. You are a legend. Thank you for looking down at me and Fa'amao that week and the months that followed to make sure we both honored your legacy.

One of our final meetings was John, Carl, and me meeting with the American Samoa EPA staff to give them an all-hands. I thanked them for all the good work they did. I let them know much had been accomplished over the week. I underscored that while we lost their leader, Ameko, Fa'amao had stepped into his shoes, and I felt confident he would not let them or Ameko down.

I let them know what I sincerely felt. In a very bizarre way, the passing of Ameko had created a situation that had brought us all much closer together than the originally planned trip would have. I had gained so much respect for Fa'amao and his staff in how they responded, and I believed they felt the same way about this rookie R9 RA.

And then John and I met with the American Samoan EPA general counsel, Marian McGuire. Ms. McGuire had been in the states during the week and had returned on Wednesday night. John and I entered the conference room. She started out by thanking me. She had been briefed about what had transpired over the previous four days. She especially thanked me for standing up for American Samoa EPA and Fa'amao with the governor and his staff. She said she would start reaching out to our staff to start revisiting the CD.

I then told her I was glad she was there to take the lead as an attorney to assist Fa'amao with the task force, and then I mentioned that the chair of the task force, AG Salo Ale, seemed to be a person who would definitely be anyone's match. I joked, "Who wears such an expensive Armani business suit in American Samoa at a meeting?" She joked back, "My husband." Attorney General Salo Ale was also her husband. I thought, *American Samoa, where everyone knows and is related to someone.*

At the end of the day, American Samoa received the modifications they needed in the CD, and they can thank Fa'amao and a husband-and-wife combination for it, Ms. McGuire and Mr. Salo Ale, the general counsel of American Samoa EPA and the then attorney general and now lieutenant governor of American Samoa.

I left thinking how wonderful American Samoa and its people were. I came to know that all the Pacific Island territory people were some of the most humble, gracious, appreciative, and patriotic Americans I had ever met anywhere. At Governor Moliga's invitation, I was going to attend the American Samoa Flag Day in 2020, but then COVID hit, and all travel into and out of American Samoa was stopped. But I can assure you that my wife and I will be in American Samoa for a future Flag Day holiday to visit an incredible US territory that has incredible, loving people.

My first trip to one of my three Pacific Island territories was completed. My first CRTF annual meeting was also a thing of the past. I believed that on both fronts, everyone saw an RA who was tested but did not waver when it came to his commitment to serve the mission of the EPA to protect human health and the environment.

Hopefully, this book and, certainly, the story of successfully modifying the StarKist CD underscore a theme I have tried to live by in my various political capacities: You don't have to be against the economy to be for the environment, and you don't have to be against the environment to be for the economy. You can be for both. That was the perspective I brought to the job every day I served as the R9 RA.

Week 13 was over. I was headed home, and my first one hundred days were behind me. I would start the following week in Arizona, my fifth trip to the state in just over one hundred days on the job.

CHAPTER 5

The EPA versus California

MANY REPORTERS, POLITICAL APPOINTEES, individuals within the Presidential Personnel Office (PPO), members of Congress, and friends have speculated as to the real reasons why Administrator Wheeler terminated me. Some reporters even speculated that my close working relationship with Speaker Pelosi led the president to order my firing. It was well known that I had a letter from Speaker Pelosi thanking me for restoring the confidence, integrity, and transparency of the EPA in regard to the Hunters Point Superfund site.

As a result of that letter, which was also well known for hanging in my office in San Francisco, reporters suggested it was no coincidence that I was terminated at 8:00 a.m. in such a bizarre way the morning after the president's State of the Union Address, during which Speaker Pelosi tore up the speech. These reporters actually had me starting to believe this scenario until I received a call from the PPO about three weeks later advising me that the president was very unhappy with my termination and wanted to send a message to Wheeler about his dissatisfaction by appointing me to a new position. The conversations that followed ultimately led to me being appointed by the president as US representative to the Western Interstate Energy Board.

So while only Andrew Wheeler, Doug Benevento, and Ryan Jackson know the real reason for my termination, I have always felt it had to do with pushback from me on certain important issues or that it related to plans Wheeler had with regard to the state of California. The fact is, I had a president who woke up every morning wanting to take a shot at Governor Newsom, and Governor Newsom woke up every morning wanting to take a shot at President Trump.

I strongly believe that Administrator Wheeler took ill-advised actions with California solely to ingratiate himself with the president knowing how the president felt about Newsom and California. It is only my opinion, but I believe many of these actions clearly violated Administrator Wheeler's oath at best and his ethical obligations or the law at worst.

Why is California so high stakes? What follows is a discussion of three contentious issues involving the EPA and California. These issues are the fuel economy standards rule, the pending state implementation plans submitted to EPA from California Air Resources Board pursuant to the Clean Air Act, and Region 9's enforcement action against the city of San Francisco in regard to stormwater discharge into San Francisco Bay, which is in violation of the Clean Water Act.

I chose to place this section of the book here, after "The First 100 Days," because this chapter focuses not only on what I believe were the real issues for my termination but also on what were, in essence, the last one hundred days of my service with the EPA. These chapters essentially focus on the months of September, October, and November 2019. As a result of these controversial issues involving the state of California and the EPA, the actions EPA took, and how I responded, by December, the die had been cast, and I am sure Wheeler and Benevento had decided I had to go. The only question was when to pull the plug.

The Safer Affordable Fuel-Efficient (SAFE) Vehicles Rule

Let me first discuss the fuel economy standards rule and the rulemaking process. As stated in "The First 100 Days" chapter, the fuel economy standards issue came up on my third day on the job in a phone conversation with Bill Wehrum, who was then the assistant administrator for the Office of Air and Radiation (OAR). Before discussing that conversation, let me give a brief overview of the fuel economy standards issue and the nature of the disagreement between EPA and the state of California.

The Obama administration fuel economy rules called for a roughly fifty-five miles per gallon average for cars by 2025. The Trump administration started the rulemaking process to implement new rules, hoping to freeze that number to around thirty-nine miles per gallon. At stake for California was a decades-old waiver from the EPA that allowed California to set its own, stricter emissions standards, which a dozen other states also follow. The proposed new rule revoked that waiver, thereby creating a national uniform standard for all states. The revocation of that waiver led to a legal showdown with California with the state arguing the EPA could not revoke the waiver.

To circumvent the rule in the revocation of the waiver, Mary Nichols, chairwoman of the California Air Resources Board, in July 2019, negotiated independently with four of the nation's largest automakers an agreement wherein they would voluntarily boost fuel economy in their fleets beginning in 2021, eventually reaching about fifty miles per gallon by the 2026 model year. The four auto companies were BMW, Ford, Honda, and Volkswagen.[4]

In a letter sent on September 6, 2019, to Mary Nichols, the EPA and the Department of Transportation advised her that the agencies took the position that the agreement was null and void as it "[appeared] to be inconsistent with Federal law." The letter also stated that pursuant to the Clean Air Act, only the federal government had authority to set tailpipe pollution standards. In response to the letter, Mary Nichols posed a question: Why would the admin-

---

[4] Information regarding the agreement between the major auto-dealers and the CA Air Resources Board:

      https://ww2.arb.ca.gov/news/california-and-major-automakers-reach-groundbreaking-framework-agreement-clean-emission.

istration oppose automakers "voluntarily making cleaner, more efficient cars and trucks and EPA [wanted]?"[5]

On May 27, 2020, California and nearly two dozen other states filed suit against the Trump administration, arguing that the EPA's decision to weaken fuel economy standards for cars and trucks put the public's health at risk and was based on flawed science. In a brief filed with the court of appeals, those challenging the rule stated the following:

> At every turn in their quest to eliminate state authority and set greenhouse gas zero emission vehicle standards, EPA and NHTSA reached beyond their own authorities, casually setting aside decades-long interpretations and practices approved by courts, disregarded statutory text and history that clearly establish congressional intent, ignored the record, and flouted core procedural requirements of the administrative law.

This matter is still making its way through the court system and could ultimately end up before the US Supreme Court. With a new administration in place, however, that is sympathetic to those who challenged the actions of the EPA and NHTSA. The parties involved may well resolve the conflict administratively.

With this background, let's return to my day three phone conversation with Bill Wehrum. The week before being sworn in, I reached out to a friend and key Democratic environmental lawmaker who was very close to Chairwoman Nichols and asked him a hypothetical question. At that point, it was widely known I would be sworn in as the next Region 9 administrator the following Monday. With my new role about to begin, I asked my friend whether, given that California could lose the lawsuit, a compromise in the fuel economy standard regarding the miles per gallon average was a possibility.

---

[5] Letter from Nichols to Wheeler: https://ww2.arb.ca.gov/sites/ default/ files/2019-10/10918_ MDN_EPA_SIP%20response.pdf.

I posed three scenarios that could ultimately result from the conflict between California and the EPA over fuel economy standards. In the first, the EPA would prevail; and nationwide, the miles per gallon average would be thirty-nine. In the second, California would partially prevail with the waiver applying only to California and not the twelve other states that had adopted California standards.

Under that scenario, forty-nine states would be using the thirty-nine miles per gallon average, and only California would use the fifty-five miles per gallon average. The third scenario would allow California and the twelve other states to have the higher standard of fifty-five miles per gallon while the other thirty-seven states would have the lower standard of thirty-nine.

Given these three potential scenarios, I asked my friend if, from his environmental perspective, California could use the clout of their waiver to get a uniform national standard higher than thirty-nine but lower than fifty-five applicable to all fifty states. Would that not be an environmental win versus, at best, thirteen states having the higher environmental standard with the strong possibility that no states would? I had no idea what a potential middle ground between fifty-five and thirty-nine would be, but I wanted to know if there would be any interest in California exploring that scenario.

My friend quickly responded yes and that if EPA were interested, he would be more than happy to be a liaison to Mary Nichols to discuss a potential middle ground. Keep in mind the timing of this conversation. The rulemaking process had just started, as had the rhetorical give-and-take between the EPA and the state of California, primarily through the California Air Resources Board and Chairwoman Nichols. The public hearings would not take place until September 2018, four months later. The rulemaking process would take years, which was why the actual lawsuits were not filed until May 2020. If there was going to be any time for compromise, this was it. Keep in mind, too, that this was on day three on the job.

As discussed in the prior chapter, I was driving up to Lake Arrowhead to make my first public appearance, addressing the California agricultural commissioners at their annual meeting. My chief of staff, Amy Miller, was driving so that I could have my conversation with Mr. Wehrum. I was actually looking forward to the call, thinking a potential roadmap to settlement and compromise with California would be something enthusiastically welcomed and embraced. That expectation couldn't have been further from the truth.

I told Mr. Wehrum that I had numerous contacts on the Democratic side of the aisle in the California State Legislature and that I believed the opportunity to meet California in the middle would be something California would be open to considering. I naively believed this was an opportunity that Mr. Wehrum would be excited about, as I knew the automobile industry was lukewarm at best with this proposed rule. My assessment would obviously bear out to be fact when Mary Nichols announced a deal with the automobile industry some fourteen months later.

This conversation, however, was very short. Mr. Wehrum said he looked forward to meeting me in person when I visited DC in July, a month and a half later. As for a potential discussion of a potential compromise with the state of California, Mr. Wehrum said he would get back to me if there was any interest at all in pursuing the possibility. We both hung up.

I looked at my chief of staff, who had been listening to the conversation on speakerphone, and I told her it was clear from Mr. Wehrum's voice that he had no interest in taking any time in potentially discussing a compromise. I told her how disappointing his approach and response to a compromise was for me. I told her we had the possibility of finding a balancing point where the economy and the environment could win, the state of California could win, and the EPA and the Trump administration could win as well. That possibility, however, seemed to have been lost on Wehrum. A great opportunity had been squandered. She agreed with me on all points.

Before leaving this topic, let me share with you my personal feelings regarding the fuel economy standard issue. Personally, I felt that pursuing rulemaking to change the fuel economy standards never made much sense. First, the automobile industry never really embraced the process. For all the heat the president and the EPA took from the opposition, they deserved to have full support from the industry, which would benefit from the change of rules. That never happened.

And as previously discussed, two-thirds of the way into the rulemaking process, the largest automakers went around the administration and EPA and cut a deal with California. It was obvious from the outset that the industry was never going to rally with passion for the proposed changes. Consequently, it never made sense to me to take so much heat over a controversial subject when the benefactor, essentially, couldn't care less.

Second, as a practical matter, the fuel economy standards will be driven by the consumer, and the higher MPG standard will be demanded by the consumer, notwithstanding wherever the EPA fuel economy standard lands. Keep in mind that EPA's target was thirty-six miles per gallon standard in the year 2025. I believe any objective assessment of consumers for new automobiles clearly shows a demand that today almost exceeds thirty-six miles per gallon. By 2025, it would not surprise me if, to meet consumer demands, the automobile industry average for new automobiles being sold will exceed the fifty-five miles per gallon from the Obama rule.

It was because of this reality why I believed the automobile industry never really cared. They knew the standard would be met because of consumer demand alone. I can only say, shame on the automobile industry for allowing a president and the president's EPA to take so much heat for an issue they initially claimed to care about when, in fact, they couldn't care less.

Finally, in regard to the fuel economy standard rule, the EPA held three public hearings throughout the country. The first was in Fresno, followed by Detroit, and finally, in Philadelphia. I was asked to preside over the Fresno hearing. My opening statement was drafted by headquarters, which I read into the record as I started the hearing. Throughout the entire rulemaking process, I never voiced my skepticism about the ruling to the public. On the contrary, I felt that any good presidential appointee should stand by the decisions and policies of their president.

A week before the hearing, in a meeting with then CalEPA secretary Matt Rodriguez, we joked over the fact that high-level appointees appointed by governors and presidents often might not personally support the policies they were asked to promote. Like an attorney representing his or her client, you make the argument that represents your client's best interest. In the case of a presidential or gubernatorial appointee, it is not your place to second-guess your boss, the governor or president, in regard to decisions, policies, or the agenda. Indeed, this is the first time I have spoken out publicly expressing my personal belief that this rule should never have been pursued.

Syringes in the San Francisco Bay

On the morning of Thursday, September 19, 2019, I awoke to read various news accounts about the president commenting on an issue with which I had been fully engaged. That issue was the serious violations of the Clean Water Act by the city of San Francisco in regard to stormwater drainage and runoff in the San Francisco Bay. The president, after touring the wall at the US-Mexico border, at the end of the day on Wednesday, the eighteenth, made claims to the press pool that discarded drug needles were making their way through the city's sewage system and into San Francisco Bay in the Pacific Ocean. The president specifically stated the following:

> You know, there's tremendous pollution being put into the ocean because they're going through what's called the storm sewer that's for rainwater. And we have tremendous things that we don't have to discuss pouring into the ocean. You know there are needles, there are other things. It's a terrible situation in Los Angeles and San Francisco. And we're going to be giving San Francisco—they're in total violation—we're going to be giving them a notice very soon. You're going to see over the next, I would say, less than

a week. EPA is going to be putting out a notice.
They're in serious violation.

Reading the news accounts the following morning, I couldn't help but think that the shit was definitely now going to hit the fan. Before proceeding, let me take you back to six weeks earlier. In early August, I met with my regional counsel, Sylvia Quast, and Amy Miller, who was now my enforcement division director, to discuss the situation regarding stormwater runoff into San Francisco Bay and the Pacific Ocean.

For over a year, Region 9 staff had been in negotiations with the city of San Francisco regarding serious violations of the Clean Water Act via stormwater discharge into the bay and ocean. I told Ms. Quast and Ms. Miller that negotiations had been going on for far too long without a settlement. It was time to play hardball.

We discussed the situation, and I said we should work with the Department of Justice (DOJ) and file a notice of violation (NOV) and a civil complaint in the US district courts for violations of the Clean Water Act. They both agreed with my assessment, and pursuant to protocol, they advised headquarters of our intention to pursue this matter as an enforcement action. Headquarters had no objection to our decision and gave us the green light to proceed.

It is important to note that EPA policy prohibits any EPA employee from publicly commenting on an enforcement action. Indeed, going back to September 18, after the president's comments, when Administrator Wheeler was asked to comment, he correctly stated, "I can't comment on potential enforcement actions." Unfortunately, as will be discussed shortly, our administrator, shortly thereafter, forgot about the enforcement action comment policy.

Back to early August. Leading up to our meeting, all parties participating in the negotiations for settlement were taking the settlement meetings very seriously. It was my assessment, as well as that of Quast and Miller, that the parties involved would be taking the negotiations even more seriously if we moved ahead with a civil complaint filed by the DOJ and an NOV issued by me. That all changed on September 18, when the president made his comments regarding stormwater discharge into San Francisco Bay, saying his EPA was going to take enforcement action within days.

Just as Attorney General William Barr expressed on several occasions his own disappointment over comments made by President Trump regarding pending actions at the DOJ, I was disappointed the morning of the nineteenth when I read what the president had stated. The bottom line, whether it was a pending matter for Attorney General Barr or an enforcement action for me, the president making any comments that prejudiced the case made settlement more difficult to achieve. When I read the comments, I knew that the same parties that had been taking negotiations seriously and in good faith henceforth would consider the issue purely political because of the president's comments.

The president is the president, and he is entitled to say whatever he wants. Again, as a presidential appointee, I never publicly criticized the president for those comments. After reading the comments, I discussed the situation with Quast and Miller and told them it was clear headquarters had briefed the president down to the details of my intentions to issue an NOV. We discussed how unfortunate the situation was, as we believed our regional staff and I had the issue well in hand and had laid a course of action that would lead to a settlement to the benefit of all parties.

Given the president's comments, we all agreed that whatever action we would now take would be deemed political and in response to the president's comments. Nothing could be further from the truth, but we knew that would be a conclusion to which many people would arrive, including Governor Newsom. So much for the president and his comments. Back to Administrator Wheeler and how soon he forgot the EPA's no comment policy regarding enforcement actions.

On September 26, 2019, eight days after the president made his comments and Wheeler said he couldn't comment because it was a pending enforcement action, Wheeler not only sent a letter to Governor Newsom regarding the issue but he also had the EPA issue a formal press release. Both the letter and the press release clearly violated the EPA's no comment rule. I urge the reader to read both the press release and the letter to Governor Newsom in the appendix.[6] In any event, like the morning of September 19, when I woke up to read the president's comments to my surprise, I woke up the morning of September 26 even more surprised. Reuters reported the following that morning:

> The Trump administration's environmental regulator escalated its feud with California on Thursday, accusing the state of violating clean water laws by allowing human waste from home-less residents to enter waterways, according to a letter it sent to the state's governor. The letter from Trump's EPA is the latest clash of many between the Republican president and Democratic offi-cials who lead the most populous US state. The issues have ranged from policy disputes to legal challenges around immigration, automobile effi-ciency and housing.

Reuters's report went on to quote Wheeler in regard to actions he intended to pursue if San Francisco and California did not respond. Again, in my opinion, this clearly violated the EPA's no comment rule. I have found that the most blatant violation of this rule is the press release issued by the EPA regarding the subject matter, which, again, I urge the reader to read.

It is one thing for the president to say what the president wants. Administrator Wheeler, on the other hand, was totally out of line, in my opinion, and in violation of the oath we took and of the no comment rule when he acted as he did on the twenty-sixth.

On October 2, 2019, I issued the NOV to the San Francisco Public Utilities Commission for violating the National Pollutant

---

[6] Letter from Wheeler to Newsom: https://sanfrancisco.cbslocal.com/wp-content/uploads/sites/15116056/2019/09/epa2.pdf.

    Press Release from EPA: https://www.epa.gov/newsreleases/epa-administrator-wheeler-calls-out-californias-environmental-protection-failure.

Discharge Elimination System permit. In the NOV, I stated the following:

> For example, lack of proper operation and maintenance has caused main and pump station failures that have diverted substantial volumes of raw and partially-treated sewage to flow across beaches and into San Francisco Bay and the Pacific Ocean. There have been instances of sewage flowing in the streets and entering people's homes. Moreover, the city's data also shows other pollutants of significant concern such as copper, zinc, lead, cyanide and ammonia that can threaten the water quality of the Bay in the ocean.[7]

Unlike Administrator Wheeler, when I was contacted by the media for comments on October 2 and in the days that followed, I responded, consistent with the EPA's no comment policy comment, "I can't comment on this matter, as it is a pending enforcement action. The NOV speaks for itself."

As for the administrator and typical of several matters discussed in this book, he never consulted with me regarding his intended actions and never sought out my opinion or gave me a heads-up of what to expect despite the fact that these were hot-button issues in my region. This behavior lined up with what regional administrators had complained about to me in personal conversations. Wheeler had taken a controversial action in my region and left me to read about it in the newspaper for the first time.

Again, I never publicly expressed my dissatisfaction. I just continued to play with the hand that headquarters and the administrator dealt to me. One thing was for sure. If the president's comments weren't enough for those on the other side of the negotiation table

---

[7] The NOV I issued 10/2/2019: https://www.epa.gov/ca/city-and-county-san-francisco-npdes-compliance-information.

to perceive the EPA's actions as solely political, the administrator's action certainly sealed the deal on that front.

By October 2, when I issued the NOV, I think any observer, other than those of us in Region 9 who had been working on the San Francisco Bay stormwater issue, believed my NOV was nothing more than a presidential political appointee following the directive of the president, as he forewarned would happen on September 18. In actuality, there were no politics involved for me or anyone else involved with the issue in Region 9. We were only fulfilling our duties and obligations in carrying out our responsibilities in enforcing the Clean Water Act. But thanks to the comments of President Trump and the subsequent actions taken by Administrator Wheeler, no objective observer would accept that our actions were anything but political.

In reflecting back on what transpired that September, I am not sure the president can be faulted, as it would not surprise me if those from EPA and others in the White House who briefed him on the subject matter did not underscore for the president why he should not comment on the pending EPA enforcement action. I don't know that for a fact, but based on how things transpired at the time, that was my conclusion.

As for Administrator Wheeler, I can only conclude that he so recklessly violated the EPA's no comment rule regarding enforcement actions because he wanted to ingratiate himself with the president given the president's comments a week before he took the actions he did. I strongly believe that he did not have direction from the president or the White House to issue the press release or write the letter to Governor Newsom. Again, I don't know this for a fact, but that was the conclusion I drew based on everything I knew at the time.

And one more thing. I have no idea why the president concluded that the EPA had found syringes in the bay. While Region 9 did find evidence of all the things referenced in my NOV, syringes were not among them. I guess the issue of syringes in the bay is something only the president or Administrator Wheeler thought should be added to their narrative of what was, in fact, an environmentally disastrous situation involving San Francisco stormwater drainage into the bay and the ocean.

To this day, I believe the matter would have been settled within six months of my meeting in August with Quast and Miller. Because of the actions taken by the president and, more importantly, by Administrator Wheeler, the matter became so political that settlement on the matter was still pending when President Biden was sworn in. With a new administration and a fresh start on settlement discussions, I believe a settlement will occur in the immediate future.

Before leaving this subject matter, there is something that needs to be disclosed to set the record straight. On October 15, 2019, the *New York Times* wrote a story regarding this subject matter entitled, "EPA Bypasses Its West Coast Team as Feud with California Escalated."[8] I can't remember who in the Office of Public Affairs called to advise me that the administrator was concerned about the story and wanted a quote from me saying that I had been advised about the letter he sent to Governor Newsom and that I fully supported the contents in the letter.

I told the individual that I couldn't do that as I was not asked for my opinion and was never shown the letter in advance to give my comments, that I believed the letter was inaccurate, and that I learned about it by reading the *Los Angeles Times*. I told him that the most I could do, especially since this was an enforcement issue, was state that I was aware of the situation and that it was very serious. Quoting the article verbatim in the relevant parts, it stated the following:

> "Unlike previous administrations that were complacent with noncompliance, this administration will not let these serious environmental failures languish," said Michael Stoker, the administrator of EPA Region 9, which includes California. He added that he was aware of Mr.

---

8   *New York Times* article: https://www.nytimes.com/2019/10/15/climate/epa-trump-california.amp.html?0p19G=2103.

Wheeler's letter before it went out and agreed that it was warranted.

All quotes were given directly from the Office of Public Affairs to the *New York Times*. I never spoke to the reporter or anyone else with the *New York Times*. Significantly, the first quote of the article was accurate, which I had given my permission to provide. The unquoted, added section was evidently given by the Office of Public Affairs and was a downright lie, and whoever gave that information knew it was false from my earlier conversation stating I could not provide what Administrator Wheeler wanted. When I read the article, I could only conclude that what Administrator Wheeler wanted in the *New York Times* article was going to happen, whether true or not and with or without my permission.

State Implementation Plans (SIPs) and the State of California

I have no idea what side of the bed Administrator Wheeler woke up on to start the week of September 20, 2019, but it was definitely on the side of anything goes when taking on the state of California. We already discussed the press release and the letter that went out from EPA and Wheeler on September 23 regarding stormwater run-off issues into the San Francisco Bay and the Pacific Ocean. As I read about the administrator's actions in the newspaper, I had no idea this was only round one. Round two would take place the very next day, on September 24.

On the morning of September 24, 2019, after drinking my morning cup of coffee, I logged on to my EPA computer to check my emails. One of the first emails I saw was a press release from the EPA entitled, "EPA Takes Action to Assure California Meets Nation's Air Quality Standards." The day before, on September 23, it was EPA versus California in regard to the Clean Water Act. Evidently, from the title of the press release, on September 24, it would now be, "EPA versus California in regard to the Clean Air Act."

The press release started out by stating the following:

> Yesterday, U.S. Environmental Protection Agency (EPA) sent a letter to California Air Resource Board (CARB) Chairman Mary Nichols notifying her of the Trump Administration's forthcoming action to eliminate its backlog of California State Implementation Plans (SIPs). This action is a necessary step towards ensuring compliance with EPA's National Ambient Air Quality Standards (NAAQS) designed to ensure that all Americans have clean air.

I will not go into much greater detail regarding the press release other than to say that the general theme was California not living up to its basic responsibilities under the Clean Air Act, and "as a result, millions of Californians live in areas that do not meet our nation's air quality standards." In reading the press release, the keyword, as far as I was concerned, was *letter*, which was highlighted, meaning you could click on it to bring up the actual letter. While there were no enforcement actions pending in regard to this issue and, therefore, no policies prohibiting the administrator from discussing the issue in public, I could only think, "Here we go again." I then proceeded to click on the word *letter*.

While the September 24 press release referenced the letter being sent the day before, the first thing I noticed in reviewing the letter was that it, too, was dated September 24, 2019. Before discussing the letter, for those of you not familiar SIPs, let me briefly explain what they are.

A SIP is a collection of regulations and documents used by a state, territory, or local air district to reduce air pollution in areas that do not meet National Ambient Air Quality Standards. Failure to carry out the SIP responsibility correctly, including submitting timely and approvable plans to assure attainment of the NAAQs, can put at risk the health and livelihood of millions of Americans.

The SIPs can be major or minor in their detail. Major SIPs outline significant actions to be taken by the air district to meet the NAAQS and also include key ozone NAAQS attainment plans. Minor SIPs often pertain to less significant actions with regard to an air district's rules. In any event, back to the letter.

The letter proceeded to blast and accused the state of California of being derelict in its duties in processing the SIPs, alleged that many of the SIPs were attainment plans, and stated that of the 130 SIPs in backlog, the vast majority "appear to have fundamental issues related to approve ability, state requested holds, missing information or resources."

Upon finishing the letter, I could only think, *Who advised the administrator with regard to the California SIP issues and the allegations raised in the letter?* They were clearly not factual. My next action was to call up my Region 9 air division director, Elizabeth Adams, to ask her if she or anyone on our air division staff had coordinated with headquarters in writing the letter. She advised me, "Absolutely not."

In our discussion, I expressed my frustration with what now had become the common experience of Administrator Wheeler in sending letters, issuing press releases, or making public comments about controversial issues in my region without seeking out my opinion or advice, deciding it would always be better for me to read about it in the newspaper.

Why Administrator Wheeler made it a common practice, I'll never know. What I do know is, I worked for two people. I worked for the president, and I worked for Administrator Wheeler. My job, as was the job of all regional administrators, was to publicly support whatever final decision was made by either man. And while I always publicly supported all these actions, on which I was not consulted first, I believe it would have benefited all parties had I been allowed to at least give my input and the reasons for my recommendation. I concluded my conversation with Ms. Adams, suggesting we do nothing, as we were never asked for our input in drafting the letter. In my mind, headquarters and Administrator Wheeler owned the factually incorrect letter.

On October 9, 2019, Chairman Nichols responded to Wheeler's one-and-a-half-page letter with a nine-page letter of her own. Without going into great detail regarding all the specifics Nichols raised in her letter, which you can read for yourself in the appendix, the letter concluded with this:

> As shown above, CARB has been a good partner to the US EPA. California has fully fulfilled its obligations. In these circumstances—with a decade-long record of state cooperation and innovation on SIPs, steadily improving air quality, and a backlog problem solely of the US EPA's making—a threat of disapproval and imposition of sanctions constitutes an abuse of US EPA authority.
>
> As you are doubtless aware sanctions may be imposed only after extensive notice-and-comment processes and formal disapproval. Even then, the clean air act and controlling US EPA regulations generally direct that sanctions be imposed only after 18 months and if the state does not cure the issue. As a result, since the US EPA has not even proposed any such findings, sanctions would not apply until well after the US EPA's backlog could be cleared.
>
> Moreover, highway sanctions are a disfavored initial option in the rare cases where sanctions are appropriate at all. Far better would be for our agencies to continue to work to resolve the issues as the sanctions would be wasteful in a direct hit to construction jobs.

Let me briefly comment on the working relationship between Region 9 and CARB and Chairwoman Nichols. As for the working relationship, it is my opinion that the staff of Region 9 and CARB have an outstanding relationship and work very well together in solving problems that involve both agencies. As for Chairwoman Nichols, I have found her very professional, transparent, accessible, and always willing to sit down in good faith to work out a problem.

As for the two letters, let me just say that the EPA letter, without any input from Region 9, was factually incorrect. The CARB letter was 100 percent factually correct and pointed out a serious problem that EPA leadership, including the leadership in Trump's EPA, failed to address, which was the reason why the SIP backlog existed at all.

The reason for the SIP backlog will be discussed in much more detail in a coming chapter discussing the future challenges for the EPA. Let me take the time now, however, to briefly describe the reason here, as it is pertinent to the subject matter at hand.

Every year, the EPA conducts an internal resource allocation assessment regarding full-time equivalents (FTEs) and the needs between the ten regions and headquarters. For the air divisions between the regions, the EPA internal assessment for Region 9 in 2018 showed that Region 9 was short of seventy-nine FTEs based on need and demand. In October 2019, the internal assessment showed that Region 9 was short of eighty-one FTEs.

The reason Region 9 was short on FTEs in the air division was primarily due to the number of SIPs they processed every year in relationship to the other nine regions. On average, Region 9 processes over one hundred SIPs a year. As I recall from memory—again, keep in mind that all my personal notes were taken from me and never returned—Region 8 processes the second-highest number of SIPs per year, averaging approximately forty-seven SIPs. After Region 8, the average number of SIPs processed by the remaining eight regions is approximately nineteen per year.

Obviously, there is a huge workload differential between Region 9 and the other nine regions when it comes to processing SIPs. A year prior to the Wheeler letter to Nichols, I advocated at the headquarter level for a reallocation of FTEs to Region 9 to address this very issue. The acting director of the Office of Air and Radiation (OAR), Benevento, and Wheeler were all very aware of this issue. Again, this issue will be discussed in much greater detail later in the book. However, the irony I found in the situation was that Republicans who liked to give the speech of running the government like a business failed miserably at shifting FTE resources from regions that did not have as great a need to regions that did.

Back to the situation at hand. As discussed previously, my Region 9 air division director and I agreed that there was no reason to intervene with headquarters with regard to the factually incorrect letter from Wheeler to Nichols. That all changed when I received a phone call from Doug Benevento in October—I believe it was in mid-October—telling me the administrator was outraged that Nichols refused to acknowledge the problem or to take any action regarding the 130 SIPs in California.

This was the first conversation I had with anyone from headquarters since the issue first came up, when I read the Wheeler letter in the EPA press release from September 24. What proceeded to take place in my phone conversation with Benevento I found shocking and outrageous.

Specifically, Benevento suggested that I disapprove of SIPs to demonstrate to Nichols how serious the administrator was on this issue. I immediately responded to Benevento that no one from headquarters had reached out to me, my air division director, or anyone else in Region 9 to get the facts for the purpose of writing the letter to Nichols in the first place. I then told Benevento that whoever briefed Wheeler was 100 percent incorrect in the facts that were relayed to the administrator.

I advised Benevento that there were no outstanding major SIPs contrary to what had been alleged in the letter and that as a result of the severe lack of FTEs in the air division of Region 9, of which he was well aware, the EPA had actually caused the pileup of SIPs and not the California Air Resources Board. Benevento essentially told me he did not care and wanted me to take action to disapprove SIPs anyway. I told Benevento I couldn't do that. We concluded the phone conversation with me promising Benevento I would do an assessment of all 130 California SIPs to give him an actual assessment of each one and whether there were any that the EPA, meaning me, could disapprove in good faith.

Over the next month, several telephone conversations were scheduled with Benevento that included my senior policy adviser, Charles Munoz, and my air division director and her deputy. (I found it questionable why the assistant administrator, Anne Idsal, for the Office of Air and Radiation for the US EPA was not present in these calls. When I inquired about that fact with Benevento, she was fortunately included in the next meeting.) From the assessment we had done, it was clear that essentially, only one SIP was waiting for action on the part of the California Air Resources Board. In doing the assessment, we concluded that we could most likely get the ARB to withdraw thirty to forty SIPs for being stale.

I believe it was in my second conversation with Benevento—I can't remember if others were on this call—that he again pushed me to disapprove SIPs. I remember asking him if he realized the ARB could not unilaterally withdraw an SIP but needed approval from the district within California that submitted it. He wasn't aware of that fact. I then asked Benevento if he realized it would take substantially more work to disapprove an SIP due to the Record of Decision (ROD) that had to be published than it would to publish an ROD to approve one? He was also unaware of that fact.

I suggested that he allow me and my staff to work with Nichols and the ARB staff to identify SIP districts that would agree to allow the ARB to withdraw. He was agitated and acted like it was important to him personally that he be able to report to Wheeler that day that we had taken action against the ARB. I told Benevento to give me thirty days and let Wheeler take a victory lap on the ARB withdrawing SIPs.

It was clear from my conversation with Benevento that the only result he wanted was a narrative in which the EPA could say Wheeler got the best of Nichols and the ARB. In other conversations, I specifically remember stating to Benevento, "I get it. Let me do my job, and Wheeler will be able to claim that Nichols and the ARB withdrew a substantial number of SIPs solely in response to the Wheeler letter of September."

In any event, we had several conversations in the month of November; and fortunately, Benevento backed off from calling for me to unilaterally disapprove SIPs for no reason. We put our emphasis into working with the ARB to withdraw SIPs. As I had initially predicted to Benevento, we were able to convince the ARB to withdraw a substantial number of SIPs. As I recall, the number was forty-three. We were able to do that in just over thirty days because of the good, working professional relationship between the ARB and the Region 9 air division staff.

In writing this book and recalling this situation, it dawned on me that this was the only situation in which I came close to having to take the position of refusing to do what headquarters had ordered. I remember that in one of my phone conversations with Benevento, I came very close to telling him that if he wanted SIPs disapproved, he would have to have Wheeler disapprove them himself. I never said it, but I certainly thought it. Fortunately, the scenario was avoided.

As of the date of my termination, I never once publicly disagreed with Wheeler or the administration on any issue, policy, or subject matter. Additionally, as will be discussed in much more detail in subsequent chapters, I certainly never disagreed with any directive that was suggested to me. As of the date of my termination, I always did what I was asked to do.

CHAPTER 6

My Journey through Facebook Posting

May 18, 2018-Being sworn in today as the 9th Region 9 Administrator for EPA. Everyone I've met is incredible. I am so fortunate to have the staff that I'll be working with. The best of the best. And special thanks to Alexis, Amy & Deborah. Truly humbling and an honor.

May 21, 2918-In Hawaii this week to assure EPA was doing everything possible to help our state and local partners in dealing with this disaster. EPA is responsible for air quality monitoring and data analysis. Our on-site team has been doing an incredible job and I am very proud of them. Had very productive meetings with the Governor, State Dept. of Health and meetings with key folks in the Emergency Operations Center both in Honolulu and in Hilo. The people most impacted by this disaster couldn't be in better hands with the federal, state and local collaborative effort underway.

June 6, 2018-I was suppose to view the Rio Salado River Project by helicopter with Senator McCain today but scheduling matters didn't allow so I was with his staff. The senator has made this project a high priority and he has my and EPA's full support. This is an incredible project on so many levels. What most of you see as a flood control channel on take off and landing into Phoenix is being transformed into the wetlands it once was. There were two wetlands projects that have taken off and thrived that received their original funding from EPA grants. I look forward as the Region 9 Administrator to helping the Senator fulfill one of his top priorities.

June 27, 2018-With Minority Leader Pelosi today at the Capitol to discuss environmental issues impacting Region 9 of the EPA. Flying home for big event tomorrow morning at Casmalia EPA Superfund site.

June 28, 2018-Big day for me personally today. In 1991 As County Supervisor I requested that the County ask the EPA to designate the Casmalia Toxic Waste Dump a Federal Superfund site. They did starting the beginning of the remediation process. Today, with EPA Administrator Pruitt, we signed a Record of Decision, which lays out the last chapter and final actions over the next 5 Years to declare the Superfund site closed. A win-win for the community and the environment. Who knew 27 years ago when I helped start the process that I would be the Regional Administrator to be instrumental in ending the process. I am very humbled and honored by today's activities.

July 25, 2018-Spent the last two days touring a proposed Superfund site (Copper Bluff Mountain located on the Hoopa Valley Tribal lands-first three pictures outdoors) and the largest Superfund site in the U.S. (The Iron Mountain Mine just outside Redding.). There was a 1 billion dollar Consent Decree with the responsible parties involved with Iron Mountain. That money helped build an incredible infrastructure on site to convert acid run off inside the mountain and the mines into safe water that can be released into the Sacramento River. At its peak Iron Mountain was discharging 6 tons of toxic metals into the Sacramento River a day. Today with our on-site waste water treatment facility, landfill and even a dam we (EPA) can convert up to 6500 gallons per minute of toxic run-off into safe water. Truly an amazing operation to witness.

August 8, 2018-Great week in Hawaii. Meeting and tour yesterday
with Congresswoman Gabbard of a state of the art Wastewater
Treatment facility substantially funded with EPA assistance. Meeting
today with Admiral Fort of the Pacific Fleet to discuss Red Hill…
the largest underground fuel storage tank system in the world.
And ended the day with a meeting with Mayor Caldwell of The
City of Honolulu. He is doing some great things for the city and
we discussed how EPA can help. Off tomorrow for American
Samoa to attend the Coral Reef T ask Force meetings.

August 15, 2018-Great week in American Samoa. Super meeting with the Governor. Toured one of four NOAA weather stations in the world monitoring CO2 and greenhouse gas emissions. Visited the Waste Water Treatment facility that was largely funded with EPA funds and helped restore the Coral Reef in the bay. And checked out our most current project connecting 600 homes to sewer and taking them off of cesspools. The next two days I'll be representing the EPA in the Coral Reef Task Force meetings

August 17, 2018-Just arrived in Honolulu flying back home. Ended the American Samoa trip representing the EPA in the Coral Reef Task Force Meeting. Had a very good meeting with Congresswoman Amaya, hiked a mile and half (video to follow) to view a traditional village wAter system, toured as's only landfill and toured wet and dry piggeries that are EPA supported and the change from traditional piggeries with EPAs support has led to almost the complete eradication of Leptospirosis in AS. Glad to be coming home for a couple days and then off to Phoenix Sunday

U.S. EPA Federal Facility Excellence in Site Reuse Award

September 24, 2018-A great day for EPA last week when I acknowledged and awarded the appropriate parties for their efforts in transforming form Mcclellan Air Force Base into an incredible residential-commercial-business development that now employs owner 17,000 people.

September 25, 2018-I was honored to preside on behalf of the EPA over the CAFE Hearings in Fresno yesterday. I had good discussions before the hearing with CA Attorney General Xavier Becerra, The Chair of CARB Mary Nichols and CA Secretary of Cal-EPA Matt Rodriguez. While we may have policy disagreements I have a great deal of respect for all three of these very dedicated public servants.

October 18, 2018-Great meetings and border tour yesterday to respond to border problems with sewage and trash from Mexico. Thank you US Border Patrol for great tour and more importantly thank you for what you do everyday putting your life's on the line to secure our border and protect the homeland. And thank you CAL EPA Secretary, Matt Rodriquez (Secretary Rodriquez has been a real leader regarding this issue)and San Diego County Supervisor Cox and the Mayors of Imperial Beach, Chula Vista, San Diego and Coronado for participating in the Stakeholders meeting I put together. Together we are all going to see a day when the border is secured environmentally and the days of trash and sewage discharges from Mexico into the US are behind us. Thank you all again.

October 23, 2018-Fighting for cleaner air. Yesterday in Fresno I First was allowed to operate the "crusher" and demolished an old diesel burning tractor as part of our buy-out program where we take old dirty burning Diesel engines out of operation and replace with cleaner newer engines.

This is a huge program in regards to helping the San Joaquin Valley reach attainment with the Federal Clean Air Standards. And then I flew in an experimental all electric plane. One of the first in the world. The next 10 years is going to blow you away in regards to all electric planes.

November 27, 2018-Great day for California agriculture today.
For over 30 years the agricultural community has advocated for the
construction of the Sites Reservoir. (I can't tell you how many speeches
I've given.). Today as Region 9 Administrator for the EPA I joined
Secretary of Interior Zinke, Secretary of Agriculture Perdue and my
good friends Congressman LaMalfa, Denham and Valadao to announce
a $440 miilion low interest loan to construct the Maxwell Water
Intertie. The event was held on the offices of Sites Project Authority
Office in Maxwell, CA. For the first time sine I can remember I
actually feel confident the Sites Reservoir is going to be built.

December 11, 2018-A great trip to Guam. Meetings with Guam EPA and Guam Water Authority who are doing an incredible job working with Region 9 of the EPA. Enjoyed the tours of the Waste Water Treatment Facility, the PFA's Treatment Facility and going down into the water aquifer for Guam's drinking water. Super meeting with the Governor and Lt. Governor Elect. And especially appreciated my meeting with Rear Admiral Chatfield (Commander of Joint Region Marianas/ U.S. Naval Forces Marianas) discussing the collaborative working relationship between the Navy and EPA. On to Saipan Thursday to review EPA projects and meet with our wonderful Emergency Response folks who have been dealing with the response to Typhoon Yutu.

December 11, 2018-Pretty incredible moment. I am sitting with Rear Admiral Chatfield at the same conference table that President Johnson sat meeting with the North Vietnamese in 1967 trying to negotiate a settlement to the Vietnam War. I am sitting exactly where President Johnson sat and Rear Admiral Chatfield is sitting. exactly where Secretary of State Robert McNamara sat. Zoom in on the picture behind us.

December 12, 2018-This trip has a special personal meaning to me. My grandfather served in WWII. He was a SeeBee and was stationed first in Guam and then Eniwetok and finally Tinian. On July 21, 1944 the Marines stormed Asan Beach pictured here. Two weeks later the combined forces retook Guam and freed the local patriotic Chomorros. My grandfather was then sent to Eniwetok and Tinian. The B 52s that dropped the Atomic bombs to end the war took off and returned to Tinian. My grandfather was there that day. My grandfather was also very artistic. He made the ring in the last picture. You see the words inscribed Eniwetok and Tinian. He left Tinian after the war in 1945. Friday I return to Tinian to review EPA's response efforts to Typhoon Yutu. I will be wearing the ring and returning to the place where it was made. I am very proud of you Grandpa Stoker. Thank you for your service and bravery to keep America free. You like your colleagues who served with you in the Pacific were truly the Greatest Generation.

December 12, 2018-Good day with my friend Governor Calvo who did incredible things in 8 years for environmental protection for Guam. Toured the now famous Dump and did some exploring and verifying in Guam harbor. Ended with a bbq with Guam EPA. They are incredible and doing an incredible job. Off to Saipan tomorrow.

December 21, 2018-After Guam it was off to Saipan to review our EPA emergency response efforts to Typhoon Yutu. The island was devastated. We're coordinating our efforts with FEMA who provide EPA our Mission Assignments. Expect to continue response through February with recovery to happen thereafter and last throughout the year. Next Friday I'll visit our Incident Command Center in Chico that was opened two weeks ago to carry out our FEMA Response Mission Assignments to the Camp Fire. We expect to be carrying out this disaster response for the next 12 months. Paradise was completely destroyed. Over 17,000 structures destroyed. The devastation is overwhelming. All our thoughts and prayers should be with all those affected by Typhoon Yutu, the Camp Fire and the Woolsey Fire who are going through a really tough holiday season. God bless them all.

December 29, 2018-I spent yesterday visiting my Region 9 emergency responders carrying out our Camp Fire FEMA Mission Assignments. These folks are truly incredible people that do so much to help a community recover. This is a nationwide response meaning emergency responders from all 9 of the other regions have been deployed to assist my Region 9 Team. First stop was the Incident Command Post in Chico followed by a tour of Paradise. The devastation is overwhelming. For all of us in southern Santa Barbara county imagine if 95% of all structures between Goleta and Carpinteria would have been destroyed in the Thomas Fire last year…that is Paradise. Please have all of those affected in the Camp Fire and our emergency responders in your hearts, thoughts and prayers.

 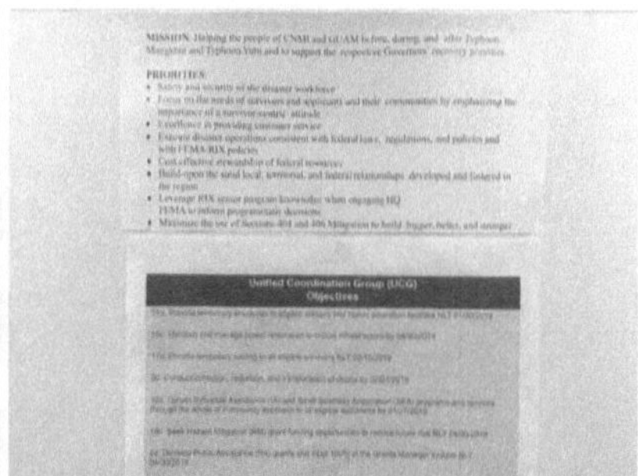

January 29, 2019-Great meeting today with my staff and Bill
Roche's (Deputy Regional Administrator Region 9 for FEMA)
staff regarding EPA's role and assistance in CNMI Typhoon
Yutu Recovery efforts. EPA Region 9 and FEMA Region 9
have a great federal partnership working relationship.

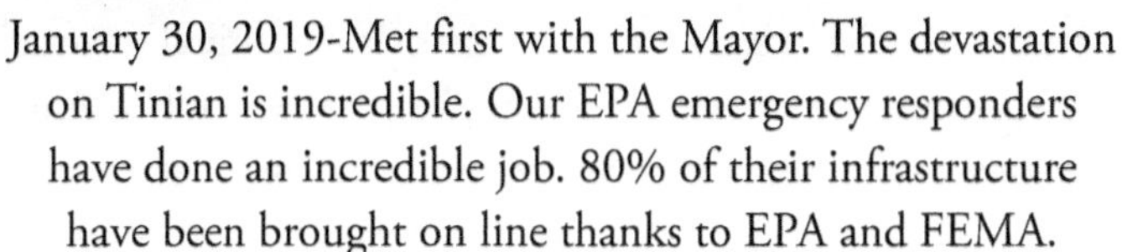

January 30, 2019-Met first with the Mayor. The devastation
on Tinian is incredible. Our EPA emergency responders
have done an incredible job. 80% of their infrastructure
have been brought on line thanks to EPA and FEMA.

February 25, 2019-Great day in DC. First meetings with the State Department far left to discuss how EPA can have much greater impact in the Pacific. Then very productive meetings at EPA Headquarters advocating for Region 9. Ended the day at the White House representing EPA at the Interagency Group on Insular Affairs focusing on the US territories. At the head table is Acting Secretary of Interior David Bernhardt (who has also been nominated by the President to be the next Secretary) and to my left Rear Admiral Chatfield who I spent time with when in Guam in early December. And yes a picture of me freezing off my buns and trying to stay warm.

February 26, 2019-Great day on Capitol Hill. Briefed Speaker
Pelosi on Superfund site Hunters Point, briefed Congresswoman
(and Presidential candidate) Gabbard on Red Hill and
Congressman Sabann from the CNMI (an American territory)
on EPA's continuing response to Super Typhoon Yutu.

March 28, 2019-Great day today. First tour of San Diego Harbor
with Harbor Commission and Harbor Patrol. Thank you both for
such a great tour. Then Border's meeting hosted by Jared Blumenfeld,
former RA of Region 9 of EPA and now Secretary of Cal-EPA.
All I can say is the Governor made a great appointment of a man
who is so know knowledgeable and passionate in regards to the
environmental issues that affect our state and nation. Together all
of us are going to get this trans boundary sewage issue solved. And
I have to end with folks I care so much about… Border Protection.
They didn't sign up to be environmental police. i want to leave this
job knowing they are no longer subjected to this threat that they
take home to their families. I'am so proud that this administration
has given so much more to protect them and secure our borders
environmentally. As long as I am the R9 Administrator eliminating
trans boundary sewage will remain one of my top personal priorities.

AMRCS Industry Day
Window Rock, AZ
April 16, 2019

DANGER
RADIATION
AREA
KEEP OUT

June 28, 2019-From an incredible wedding getting married to my true soul mate to working honeymoon in Guam. This week was the 30th Pacific Islands Conference. Meetings with Admiral Chatfield, the Assistant Secretary of the Air Force, our incredible regulatory partners with Guamanians America Samoa EPA and CNMI BECQ and so many others. A cruise with Guam EPA to check wastewater outputs and some snorkeling to check out the coral reef. (I represent the EPA on the US Coral Reef Task Force.). And an especially proud day for the government of Guam as we cut the ribbon for a brand new Wastewater Treatment Plant that will make sure that future generations have a safe and environmentally protected Ted Agat Bay. Next week honeymoon in Japan. I love you sooooo much Debi Stoker.

August 18, 2019-A lot accomplished for the EPA this last week in Hawaii. Meetings with the Governor, Honolulu Mayor Caldwell, Congressman Case, Congresswoman Gabbard and US Senator Hirono's staff, executive directors' of Hawaii Surfriders and Hawaii Community Foundation, an incredible tour of the Coral Reef Restoration Project and tour by boat of Pearl Harbor of Superfund (CERCLA) and hazardous materials (RCRA) Sites.

September 1, 2019-Great week last week for my personal priorities
(my tribes, the Pacific Islands-America Samoa, Guam, CNMI and
the Freely Associated States-and the border) as the Southwest Region
Administrator for the US EPA. Monday I hosted in San Diego a
stakeholder's meeting for developing an action plan to deal with trans
boundary sewage flow from Mexico into the US. Pictured with me is
Congressman Scott Peters and US EPA Assistant Administrator for
International & Tribal Affairs, Chad McIntosh. Tuesday I hosted in San
Francisco at our regional headquarters the US Army & Missile Defense
Command, NOAA, US Fish & Wildlife, Army Corp of Engineers. and
the Republic of the Marshall Islands to discuss EPA's environmental
compliance assistance regarding the Army's faculty on the Kwajalen Atoll.
And Wednesday and Thursday a tour in Nevada of 2 of my 148 tribes
in a Region 9…the Pyramid Lake Paiute Tribe and the Washoe Tribe.

September 4, 2019-Yesterday was a super day. I had the honor in participating in a groundbreaking of a creek restoration project funded in large part with EPA dollars. This restoration project will tie the creeks of Brentwood into the San Francisco Bay in a big way. Today's children growing up in this area will be tomorrow's adults telling stories how they grew up and played next to these creeks. A big win for the community and the environment.

September 14, 2019-Really productive week at the Annual Coral Reef Task Force Annual meeting this week in Palau. Meetings with Ambassador Amy Hyatt will pay off great dividends for the Freely Associated States. Also really good meetings with Assistant Secretary of Interior Doug Domenech, Assistant Secretary of Commerce Rear Admiral Tim Gallaudet, President of Palau Tommy Remengesau, President, Lt. Governor of America Samoa Lemanu Mauga and high governmental officials of the Republic of the Marshall Islands, Federated States of Micronesia, Territory of the US Virgin Islands, Guam, Commonwealth of the Northern Marianna Islands, Puerto Rico and the state's of Hawai and Florida. Pictures of paradise to follow.

September 30, 2019-I am so happy and proud for my good friend Robert
O'Brien for his appointment by the President to be the next National
Security Advisor to the President. Here is a picture a year ago when
Robert invited some of his close friends to watch him be sworn in at
the Treaty Room of the State Department by Secretary Mike Pompeo as
Special Envoy to the President for Hostage Affairs. The President and
America could not be better served. Robert is the best of the best and will
be an outstanding National Security Advisor. Congratulations my friend.

November 6, 2019-In Mexico City this week with EPA contingency discussing with our Mexican counterparts our next Borders Environmental understanding to deal with water, air, solid waste and emergency response mutual border issues. Great meetings. I was able to get water beneficial reuse and marine liter added as new commitments. And with some spare time to kill off to the Zocalo to revisit the incredible cathedral, view some of the highlights left over from last weekend's Life of the Living Dead festival and even buy a Panama hat for $8 American. What a deal. Home. tomorrow.

November 16, 2019-Great week this week celebrating American Recycling
Week. Tuesday at the Chumash to recognize them for their zero waste
efforts. Only 8% of what they generate ends up in the landfill. Wednesday
was with Virgo, the largest school furniture manufacturer in the world,
who have hit the incredible target of generating zero waste. And Thursday
was at CarbonLite the #1 recycler of plastic bottles in the world. And
I love their marine plastics recovery program where they are removing
marine drips from our oceans up to 30 miles offshore. Congratulations
to each of you. You are truly a role model for all to follow.

Western Regional Partnership Principals' Meeting
Marine Corps Base Camp Pendleton
November 19, 2019

December 11, 2019-My Region 9 of US EPA hosted at the Los Angeles Convention Center this week the Annual National Brownfield Conference. Me this morning giving the keynote.

Last FaceBook Post (without photos)-January 30, 2020-Today I rolled out the Trump Administration's EPA Clean Truck Initiative for the Southwest Region of EPA. For the the first time since 2001 we are taking the actions needed to make our big rig trucks cleaner burning and less emitting. Through our initiative emissions will be reduced 30% plus by 2027 which will be huge in giving us all cleaner, safer air to breath. This on top of the fact of the great job the US has done to reduce dirty air emissions by 73% since 1970

February 2, 2020-No Facebook post that day but pictures of last day on the job. Was touring the NPL Superfund site located on and around the airport in Goodyear, Arizona. I flew back to LAX. My wife Debi picked me up and we drove home. We had dinner watching the State of the Union Address by President Trump. This was the State of the Union that Speaker Pelosi tore up the speech while sitting behind the President delivering the speech. The next morning at 8 am I received the call from Mr. Ryan and Mr. Benevento that I either needed to tender my resignation by the end of business that day or I would be terminated. Having never been reprimanded verbally or in writing I told them if they would tell me the reason why I would resign. They refused to state any reason and I was terminated. Within 15 minutes my EPA cell phone was remotely disconnected. Within 30 minutes my EPA laptop was remotely disconnected. The end result of that day and their actions is this book.

CHAPTER 7

The Tribes and the Pacific Island Territories

Two of my top personal priorities as the R9 RA was attending to the needs of Region 9's 148 tribes and the Pacific Island territories of Guam, Northern Mariana Islands (CNMI), and American Samoa. The tribes and territories and their people have very much in common. First is their humility and graciousness. These are people who are so appreciative for so little.

Second is a common cultural thread to their ancestors. Their ancestries have their own history with their own indigenous people and culture. Whether it was the Diné in Navajo Nation, the Chamorro in Guam and CNMI, or the Polynesian people from the Tui Manu'a dynasties in American Samoa, the territories and tribes all have their own identity and their own independent history. As a result, the people of the tribal lands and the territories can relate to one another in a special, unique way that the rest of Americans who do not have a tribal ancestry cannot.

A third area where the tribes and territories find commonality is in their wealth. The fact is, the territories and most of our nation's tribes do not have the kind of revenues that most states have proportionate to their respective populations. Of the 148 tribes in R9, approximately 30 have gaming or casinos located on their tribal lands. Generally speaking, they are doing very well financially. The other 118 tribes? Not nearly as well.

For those 118 tribes and the Pacific Island territories, the lack of more substantial revenues means they have less to allocate to infrastructure. And in the world of EPA, compliance with laws like the Clean Water Act or Clean Air Act equates to the amount of money you can allocate to the infrastructure projects that will deliver cleaner air and cleaner water.

It was indeed this similarity between my tribes and the Pacific Island territories and the environmental challenges and the financial resources they had to address those challenges why I made their needs and concerns two of my top personal priorities as RA.

It is so important to underscore, too, that they truly shared the common trait of being so appreciative for so little. Giving Guam or Navajo Nation a grant or funding for $250,000 for a water infrastructure project would mean so much, and the gratitude expressed was so real. Giving a $4 million grant or funding to the city of San Diego for the same purpose would be a media event, smiles for the cameras, and presentation of the award with a thank-you.

I never felt the appreciation at city or county presentations of a financial award like I did with my tribes and Pacific Island territories. They were so appreciative, so grateful, so humble. They are truly wonderful people, and I thank God every day that I was given a couple of years of my life to work with them, get to know them, develop friendships I will have for life with them, and help them in meeting their environmental challenges.

The fact that the tribal members and the people of the Pacific Island territories feel this common bond was underscored at my first R9 tribal conference in October 2018. The annual tribal conference is when all the tribes come together to meet with the R9 staff. This has been an annual event since 1992. The conference brings together all federally recognized tribes and their tribal environmental staff from R9. The conference provides attendees with a forum for education, networking, and gaining professional development. And for an RA from R9 who makes tribes a personal priority, it gives the tribes an exceptional opportunity to focus on what resources they need help from R9.

When an RA has a personal priority, all the RA's R9 career staff know it. At the conference, the tribes can express what they need, what is working, and what is not working directly to the RA in front of his or her senior division staff members. That can be very powerful. I saw firsthand how hard my senior staff wanted to deliver for tribes or Pacific Island territories because they truly wanted me to succeed in my personal priorities.

On this last point, the incredible career staff at R9 are going to do their jobs whatever the RA's personal priorities are. That's what they do and do so well. Whether an RA has been appointed or not, these people carry out the mission of the EPA to protect human health and the environment with passion and true dedication every day they are on the job.

They do that whether they have an appointed RA in place or not, and they do it regardless of what the personal priorities of the RA are. But when an RA has personal priorities, they all take note. More on this later in the chapter regarding the Pacific Island territories and how the RA's personal priorities can make a huge impact. And I can tell without question that if you were to go to any one of the senior division directors and ask them what it means if their R9 RA succeeds, every one of them would say that if their RA succeeds, whether that RA is a Republican or a Democrat, conservative or liberal, then that means they and R9 have succeeded.

So back to my first tribal conference in October 2018. From my visits to twelve to fifteen tribes and from my visit in American Samoa in my first six months, I saw this commonality between the tribes and the territories. I suggested to my new COS, formerly my tribal division director, Laura Ebbert, that perhaps the tribes would want to consider inviting the Pacific Island territories to the upcoming tribal conference. Laura correctly reminded me that the annual conference was about the tribes and what they wanted. For a new RA to reach out with that suggestion could clearly be taken the wrong way and would show a lack of respect. I agreed and dropped the issue. And then the first day of the conference came.

The first session was for the tribes to meet and for them to decide what they wanted to report back during the general session that would follow to the R9 RA and staff, such as the issues, concerns, or recommendations they wanted to discuss. The general session began, and almost immediately, in the tribes' presentation was the suggestion that the tribes, acknowledging the similarity between them and the Pacific Island territories, invite the territories to participate in future tribal conferences.

I swear I never suggested this to anyone other than to Laura and to a couple others in my staff. I dropped the issue. The last thing I wanted was for a new RA, me, whose tribes were his top personal priority doing something that would look disrespectful. However, for some reason, what my gut told me made sense from six months of working with tribes and the territories, and the tribal members came to the same conclusion. The next year, representatives of the Pacific Island territories participated in the 2019 annual tribal conference. I am sure the territories will be included in all conferences going forward, and better yet, the tribes will be invited to participate in Pacific Island conferences as well.

Before leaving the subject matter of the annual tribal conference, I would like to briefly mention the Regional Tribal Operations Committee (RTOC). As previously mentioned, the RTOC is a working committee of the EPA and tribal personnel and is cochaired by an EPA representative and a tribal representative. EPA designates its RTOC representative through internal mechanisms. All tribes within R9 are considered members of the RTOC. Tribal representatives to the RTOC are selected through government-to-government communication by tribal leaders in various geographical areas within R9.

The RTOC is R9's primary vehicle, and through it, all tribes in R9 collectively have a voice in raising issues and concerns regarding the region's responses and actions to issues of concern to the 148 tribes. While the RTOC focuses more on government-to-government communications, more will be discussed later on about the federal government's responsibility in general and EPA specifically in conducting legally mandated government-to-government consultations on issues of concern to the tribes.

Suffice to say at this point that I believe the EPA and the federal government in general fall far short in living up to its legally mandated obligations to honor government-to-government consultation duties. But again, more on this later. Back to the spiritual connection between the tribes and the Pacific Island territories.

The tribes and islands had deep roots long before being exposed to Christianity or formal religions of any kind. One of the most spiritual experiences I've had in my life was the week I spent in Navajo Nation. While the tribes and Pacific Islands in modern times have adopted more modern religions, they all have historical ties to the gods of their ancestors. For instance, Catholicism is the predominant religion today in the Navajo Nation. For the Navajo's ancestors, it was the Diné.

The Diné passed through three different worlds before emerging into this world, the Fourth World, or Glittering World. The Diné believe there are two classes of beings: the Earth People and the Holy People. The Holy People are believed to have the power to aid or harm the Earth People. Since Earth People of the Diné are an integral part of the universe, they must do everything they can to maintain harmony or balance on Mother Earth.

It was this last point on harmony with Mother Earth that led to the Navajo development of the hózhó. Hózhó is the complex wellness philosophy and belief system of the Diné (Navajo). It consists of principles that guide one's thoughts, actions, behaviors, and speech.

At this point, I should offer a religious studies disclaimer. I do not profess to be well versed in understanding hózhó. What I learned, I learned from the Navajo Nation Superfund director, Dariel Yazzie, someone I truly consider my spiritual brother. What Dariel taught me was that hózhó teaches respect from a perspective of maintaining loyal reverence by offering respect to self, others, nature, spirit, animals, the Creator, and the environment. It was this last aspect of hózhó respect that directly involved me as the R9 RA.

Pursuing hózhó with regard to the environment means treating Mother Earth well so she will treat you well. Treat her badly and she will respond in kind many times over. (This is my interpretation of the meaning of hózhó.) For me and the Navajo Nation, that came down to the severe environmental damage caused in Navajo Nation from the mining of uranium. This will be discussed in much greater detail in the chapter "Superfund and Emergency Management."

For purposes of hózhó in the treatment of Mother Nature, you just need to be aware that from 1944 to 1986, nearly thirty million tons of uranium ore were extracted from Navajo lands. Many Navajo people worked the mines, often raising families in close proximity to the mines and mills. Today, the mines are closed, but a legacy of uranium contamination remains, including over five hundred abandoned uranium mines (AUMs), as well as homes, water sources, and land with elevated levels of radiation.

As I've said, there will be more on this in the chapter pertaining to Superfund. However, as far as hózhó is concerned, from 1944 to 1986, Mother Earth was raped in the Navajo Nation from the mining of uranium. No one did anything illegal, but no one knew better. But in hindsight, we now know the legacy this mining left. And from the perspective of hózhó, the people of Navajo Nation are now paying the consequences of Mother Earth responding in kind.

On a Thursday morning, as the sun was rising, Dariel took my staff and me out to an incredible view. Far out in the distance was the home he grew up in. This was one of the most spectacular places I had been in my life, and I had been to some pretty amazing places. Dariel asked if he could lead us in prayer. I said of course. We all circled and put our arms on one another's shoulders, and Dariel prayed for the Lord to help the people of the Navajo Nation. He prayed that we would all follow the course of action the Lord would want us to follow.

I then added to the prayer, praying that the Lord would show us the way to do the right thing, that he would bring relief and restoration to the people of Navajo Nation, that he would give us all the wisdom to revive Mother Nature within Navajo Nation, and that we would never repeat this mistake again.

As I said previously, this is one of the most spiritual moments I've had in my life. Dariel is a devout Catholic, and I am a devout Christian who attends Calvary Chapel of Santa Barbara. While in modern times Dariel and I have our respective Christian faiths, on that morning on those cliffs overlooking Navajo Nation, as we prayed, I believe we were moved mostly by the philosophy of hózhó and the connection to Mother Earth that it teaches us.

So with Navajo Nation, it was hózhó. Thousands of miles away, to the west, in America Samoa, it was the connection to the Tui Manu'a. The Tui Manu'a is one of the oldest titles in Samoa. The title is from the puhi te era. Traditional oral literature of Samoa and Manu'a talks of a widespread Polynesian network or confederacy (or empire) that was prehistorically ruled by the successive Tui Manu'a dynasties. There are various Tui Manu'a descent lines, many of which bear little resemblance to one another. It is a common belief, however, as part of Samoan myths and legends, that the first Tui Manu'a was a direct descendant of the Samoan supreme god, Tagaloa.

While, again, I am no expert on this subject matter, from what my American Samoan friends told me, a cornerstone of the worship of Tagaloa is the commitment to protect the islands, its resources, and its beauty. In other words, one must protect Mother Earth, again a common thread among the Pacific Island territories and the tribes. I can assure you, without exception, every tribe I visited had a historical spiritual belief in preserving and protecting Mother Earth.

Treat Mother Earth right and she will treat you right. Treat her wrong and you will surely face her wrath. So while the Navajos have hózhó, every other tribe I had personal dealings with essentially have the same belief that focused on how we react to and treat Mother Earth, as did my friends in American Samoa, Guam, and CNMI. But enough of the spirit world.

As previously mentioned, by the end of my tenure as RA, I would visit almost sixty tribes. The first were the four in the Owens Valley, which I mentioned in the chapter "The First 100 Days." The last would be the Salt River Pima–Maricopa Indian Community in Arizona. The longest visit would be in Navajo Nation, where I spent a week and put 1,200 miles on the car with my staff. This will be discussed in much greater detail in the chapter pertaining to Superfund.

For the Pacific Islands, my first visit was American Samoa, which I also discussed in the chapter "The First 100 Days." For Guam and CNMI, that would come, approximately, on the six-month mark, when I left to attend R9's emergency management to Super Typhoon Yutu that hit CNMI in November 2018.

On December 17, 2018, I left for my first visit to Guam and the Northern Mariana Islands (CNMI). To get to Guam, I would fly through Tokyo, overnight there, and then fly the next day to Guam. Upon my arrival in Tokyo, I was met by my Pacific Islands director, John McCarroll. John and I checked into our hotel, got a good night's sleep, and were off the next day back to the airport to fly to Guam.

Upon arrival in Guam, John and I were met by R9's Pacific Island territories division engineer, Carl Goldstein, at the airport. He drove us to the hotel we were staying in Guam. On this trip, I would meet with Governor Eddie Calvo; Governor Elect Lourdes Aflague Leon Guerrero, who is now governor; the administrator of Guam EPA, Walter Guerrero, and his staff; the general manager of Guam Waterworks Authority, Miguel Bordallo, and his board of directors; and Rear Admiral Shoshana Chatfield.

The agenda for this trip was to discuss with the admiral the new marine base being built in Guam and discuss the navy's financial assistance to the government of Guam for expansion of the Guam wastewater treatment facility, which would be processing the water-waste from the new base, and to discuss financial assistance to the Guam Waterworks Authority, who would be providing the fresh drinking water to the base.

I also wanted to personally thank Admiral Chatfield for the assistance from the navy for the sampling of Agent Orange on Guam. Agent Orange had been used in World War II. The navy's sampling allowed the EPA to identify hot spots, which were remediated to eliminate any threats to the public, who could inadvertently come into contact with Agent Orange. The final issue we had on my agenda for the navy was to flag the hot issue going forward for the R9 EPA and Guam EPA—the field construction of the fuel storage tanks to be built on the new marine base.

I would also tour the Guam wastewater treatment facility to appreciate the expansion that would be taking place. I would also tour water wells that were contaminated with PFAS (per- and polyfluoroalkyl) and visit a well with a PFAS water treatment facility/ process in place to remove PFAS from the water.

For the purpose of this chapter, let me just say that PFAS is a nasty toxic chemical. They have found their way into our drinking water supplies in many places around the country and in the territories. The chemical is used in fire-retardant chemicals and is used in waterproofing for clothing. It has been in our water supply for decades. Notwithstanding numerous past presidential administrations and their EPA knowing about PFAS in the water supply, all past administrations chose to do nothing about it until Trump's EPA.

Trump's EPA started the process to establish a maximum contaminant level (MCL) for PFAS. That is critical, as the EPA generally cannot assert jurisdiction over a public water system unless a chemical has an MCL. Once an MCL is established, EPA can establish the minimum level of parts per million (ppm) for that respective chemical in any water supply of the US. (I won't go into the specifics. However, in very limited situations, the EPA does have emergency authority regarding chemicals in drinking water, although an MCL has not been established pursuant to the Safe Drinking Water Act.) Now that Trump's EPA has made PFAS such a public issue, I feel certain the Biden administration will follow through with the rulemaking process to establish, once and for all, an MCL for PFAS.

You may ask yourself why past administrations, including the Obama administration, chose not to take any action to regulate PFAS. The answer is pretty simple. Once you acknowledge a problem, you own it, and you have to deal with it, just as we've had to deal with lead, copper, dioxin, mercury, and as I recall from memory, 537 other chemicals. Once an MCL for PFAS is established, it will be the 538th chemical to be monitored by the EPA in our nation's water supplies. Unfortunately, past administrations chose to ignore PFAS. Thankfully, the Trump EPA did not.

My final action before departing from Guam for CNMI was to advise Walter and his staff that R9 would be announcing an award of $14.7 million to Guam for environmental protection. Before leaving the subject of Guam, I would be remiss if I did not sing praise to Walter; his deputy, Jesse Cruz; and the entire Guam EPA staff. They are devoted, dedicated professionals who have turned many R9 EPA issues in Guam around. Like the American Samoa EPA that Ameko Pato turned around, Walter and Jesse have done the same thing with Guam EPA. And when you turn things around, it truly makes the environmental agency a true partner versus a potential adversary. Guam EPA is a true partner of the R9 EPA.

Walter and Jesse will be lifelong friends, and it was truly a pleasure to work with them. The only thing I regret that I was not able to accomplish for Guam was to get them a new EPA building. They are operating in an old building built during WWII near the Guam airport. The fact that the Guam EPA staff continue to give 100 percent day in and day out while working in that building is a testimony in itself to what kind of people they are. In whatever capacity I serve in the future, if I am in any position to make a difference, I will advocate for that new building for Guam EPA. And hopefully, someday, in the not-so-distant future, I will be standing at a ribbon cutting ceremony when they open up that new Guam EPA building for business.

I would return to Guam in June 2019 for the Pacific Islands conference. But for now, it was off to CNMI to tour some R9/CNMI Bureau of Environmental and Coastal Quality (BECQ) projects and to tour the devastating damage caused by Super Typhoon Yutu that hit CNMI with the strongest sustained winds ever to hit US land at 210 mph.

I arrived in Saipan, where the capital of CNMI is located, and proceeded with John and Carl by rental car to the BECQ offices. I had a briefing from BECQ administrator, Eli Cabrera, and his division director, Ray Masga. John, Carl, and I then drove to meet with the executive director of the Commonwealth Utilities Corporation (CUC), Gary Camacho, and some of his staff on-site at one of their newest freshwater storage tanks. We then went to the airport property to tour a PFAS contaminated water well, then off to the wastewater treatment facility, which had been badly damaged from the typhoon. Everywhere we went, we saw the devastation caused by Super Typhoon Yutu. Schools, residential and commercial buildings, and government buildings—everywhere you looked, it was like a war zone.

The next day, I would meet with the deputy regional administrator of FEMA, Bill Roche. That was a meeting I don't believe either Bill or I will ever forget. I suggested projects that should be funded by FEMA as part of recovery. Bill got agitated and defensive and said FEMA wasn't there to write CNMI a blank check. I backed off and told Bill I didn't expect FEMA to write a blank check.

To be consistent with the guidance FEMA operates from for funding projects in areas destroyed in federally declared emergencies, I said I would have my staff put together a list of projects that we believed in good faith were deserving of funding from being directly damaged from the typhoon. And I made a request that EPA, not the Army Corps of Engineers, be given the mission assignment (MA) for the recovery stage of the typhoon.

More on this to come, but it is important for readers who are not familiar with FEMA to understand that there are two phases for FEMA responding to a disaster. There is the initial phase of response, which addresses the short-term, direct effects of an incident. Response includes immediate action to save lives, protect property, and meet basic human needs. Recovery encompasses both short-term and long-term efforts for the rebuilding and revitalization of the affected community.

From the FEMA handbook, examples of recovery can focus on restoration of lifelines, such as water and electric supply, and critical facilities. Lon-term recovery can include more permanent rebuilding. From my recollection, Bill oversaw the entire response phase, which I recall was concluded after approximately seventy-five days.

Back to my conversation with Bill. I wanted the EPA to be given the recovery mission assignment. My argument was that my people worked with the main CNMI governmental agencies that would be involved with recovery. Those agencies were BECQ and CUC. I promised Bill that our list of recovery projects would meet his criteria, and I promised he would have the list within thirty days.

We finished the meeting as friends. I think Bill was impressed that I did not back down despite how strong he came down on me, and I know I left the meeting very impressed with how much Bill had a very bad situation under control, at least as much control over a situation like Saipan being devastated by a typhoon.

After the meeting, we visited the main landfill in Saipan, the Marpi Landfill. That landfill has some major environmental challenges. One of those challenges was the leachate at the landfill reaching the groundwater basin and negatively affecting the drinking water supply. I then met with CNMI's congressman, Vinnie Sablan, and then toured a planned coral nursery site in the ocean a mile off Saipan's coast.

During the three days there, I also met with some of EPA's emergency responders who had been deployed to CNMI as part of FEMA's mission assignment to EPA to collect hazardous household materials and locate and collect all downed telephone pole transformers.

As I previously mentioned, EPA is often the second most active federal agency, second only to FEMA, in responding to an emergency. In the case of CNMI and the typhoon, EPA would be active in literally going home to home to clear hazardous household wastes. By January 7, 2019, three weeks later, our emergency responders would collect and prepare for shipping over 1,100 transformers.

The night before we left, the BECQ staff hosted John, Carl, and me at a barbecue. Eli and I had first met at the Pacific Islands conference that took place in San Francisco six months earlier. During that time period, he had seen me in action and seen firsthand that I not only talked the talk but also walked the walk when it came to the Pacific Island territories, one of my highest personal priorities.

Eli, Walter, and Fa'amao all see the difference since I became the RA. They especially took note of what my staff, which was led by John McCaroll, was able to do with an RA who every career R9 employee knew wanted his Pacific Island territories given the attention, respect, and resources they deserved. In his comments before the barbecue, Eli said relations between R9 and BECQ had never been so good since my arrival. I thanked him and said how honored I was to be able to bring the priority of the territories back to the forefront in R9, and then I said that my next thirty days would be focused on delivering to Bill Roche his recovery list, which could be huge for CNMI going forward.

Our barbecue came to an end. John, Carl, and I returned to our hotel to get up early the next morning to fly home. I would return to CNMI in thirty days. I would return to find out how FEMA was going to pursue recovery for CNMI going forward.

We got home a week before Christmas. Without elaborating on my schedule between my return home and departing again for CNMI on January 24, 2019, I would be remiss to not mention two events. On December 28, 2018, I went up to Chico to visit the emergency responders to the Camp Fire. More on this in detail in the chapter "Superfund and Emergency Management." The second event that happened was a federal government shutdown on January 1, 2019. The shutdown was due to a budget impasse between the president and Congress.

In a federal government shutdown, everything literally shuts down. Within R9, only me as the administrator, my deputy RA, and my assistant RA were exempt from the absolute prohibition not to work. Literally, unless you were exempt, you could have job disciplinary actions taken against you if you worked. Cell phones and laptops were turned off by every R9 employee who was not exempt. To demonstrate how serious the no work policy is in a federal government shutdown, the only employees exempt from it was myself; my deputy RA; my assistant RA; our emergency responders who had been deployed to the Camp Fire, the Woolsey Fire, and Super Typhoon Yutu; and some of our Superfund staff.

In early January, I was supposed to be a keynote speaker at an annual environmental conference that UCLA hosted. I still wanted to attend but was told by headquarters I could only attend if I went in a personal capacity. I could not be introduced as the R9 RA, I was told, and I absolutely could not speak. I went and did not speak, and the MC introduced me in my former roles, saying that as a result of the shutdown, he could not introduce me in my current capacity. That got a laugh. Welcome to navigating through a federal government shutdown.

John and Carl were not exempt and, therefore, could not work with the shutdown. But I had promised Bill Roche the recovery list within thirty days, and that would only happen if John and Carl could work and coordinate with BECQ and CUC, the projects that should be on the list. I told my deputy RA and assistant RA to reach out to HQ and request that John and Carl be exempted so they could work on the recovery list, as the recovery list was associated with emergency management.

Since our emergency responders in the field were exempt, I argued that John and Carl should be exempt as an extension of being the emergency responders in CNMI. HQ agreed. I called John on his WhatsApp number since he had followed the rule and turned off his EPA phone. I advised him what had happened. He was elated. I asked him to advise Carl, and then I told him that as a result of the emergency management being exempt, the three of us would be returning to CNMI on January 24 to follow up with our emergency responders and, most importantly, meet with Bill Roche with FEMA to discuss the typhoon recovery phase. With that, I told him to go to work and get the list completed.

John and Carl worked on the list for the next two weeks. They worked closely with Juliette Hayes with FEMA to assure the recommended projects would meet the criteria Bill expected. We met Juliette in CNMI in December. She is an incredible woman. FEMA is extremely lucky to have her. While Bill was her boss from the outset, I sensed that Juliette was rooting for us to be successful in our advocacy for the recovery of CNMI from the typhoon.

I instructed John and Carl to work closely with Juliette to put together a list that would aggressively advocate for recovery projects with the following caveat: Every project had to have some nexus to the damage caused from the typhoon. If there was a preexisting problem that had worsened as a result of the typhoon, it should be added to the list unless Juliette suggested otherwise. In other words, I was counting on Juliette to vet projects with the understanding that we didn't want anything on the list that Bill would be able to look at and say, "I told you I am not giving you a blank check." I wanted Bill to look at our list and immediately conclude that we had honored our agreement to put the list together in good faith.

We arrived in Saipan on January 25, 2019. On the twenty-sixth, I met with Bill Roche. We had sent him the project list days earlier. At this meeting, it was as though Bill and I were best friends. He thanked me for the list, and he thanked me for delivering what I promised I would, and he said that as a result of the government of CNMI requesting that EPA be given the recovery mission assignment, EPA was going to be given that assignment.

If you recall, while I was in Hawaii, I suggested to the state officials that they request the EPA be given the ission assignment for putting real-time air monitoring results up on the EPA website for any member of the public to access. They did, and EPA was given the mission assignment. I am a quick learner. From that experience, I reached out to BECQ, CUC, and Congressman Sablan, suggesting that the government of CNMI request of FEMA that EPA be given the recovery mission assignment. They did, and we got it.

There will be much more regarding the emergency management in CNMI in the chapter pertaining to emergency managements, but let me leave you on a happy note. FEMA ultimately accepted our project list. Months later, based on that list, Congress would pass an appropriation bill pertaining to the emergency managements and funds that needed to be allocated accordingly. CNMI would be allocated the sum of $66.4 million. Of that amount, $56 million was allocated to deal with solid waste issues, which will significantly impact the problems at the landfill in Saipan. An additional $10.4 million was allocated to address clean water and wastewater treatment issues.

I flew home, and during my four-hour layover in Guam, Walter arranged to be escorted into the terminal and then for us to meet in a conference room. I met him, and we went over several matters. I let him know how happy I was that the newly elected governor, Governor Guerrero, had decided to keep Walter on as administrator of Guam EPA. During my meeting with the governor the month before, I underscored how much Walter and his staff had made a huge, positive difference with Guam EPA. Whether my input had anything to do with her decision, I have no clue. But from my perspective, she definitely made the right decision to keep Walter on.

I then caught my flight home. I would return five months later to Guam to preside over the 2019 Pacific Islands conference. I returned on a working honeymoon. I arrived in Guam on June 25, 2019. I was married on June 23, 2019. My incredible wife, Debi, came with me. She was an instant hit with the Pacific Islanders, who said she was a great First Lady of R9.

To avoid boring you, I will not get into the schedule of the conference. But I will say, that ribbon cutting event of a brand-new wastewater treatment facility in Guam built with EPA funding was my wife's second ribbon cutting event of a wastewater treatment facility. The other one was in Santa Barbara, California. When you're married to an EPA administrator, those are some of the perks of being with your spouse, hanging out at wastewater treatment facilities.

That was the last time I would visit the Pacific Island territories. I think of the territories and their people regularly. When you have the opportunity to meet such warm, friendly, and humble people, you don't forget them. And many of the people I met from the Pacific Island territories I will remember for the rest of my life.

Finally, I want to conclude this chapter with one sad factor the tribes and the Pacific Island territories have in common. In my opinion, neither the tribes nor the territories are given the respect and attention they deserve from the various federal agencies. All of them, including EPA, provide resources. However, I believe they give the bare minimum. The fact that representatives of the R9 tribes and territories were the first to call or email me to thank me for my service and tell me how much of a loss it was for them and state how appreciative they were for what I did for them is a sad commentary. I didn't give them more than they deserved. I gave them only what they deserved. When I left EPA, Governor Lolo of American Samoa sent me a letter.

As you turn your attention to the next
step in your career, I would be remiss if I did
not take this opportunity to thank you for your

service and leadership as the US EPA Region 9 Administrator. I received news of your departure from the US EPA with regret… I can assure you that your tenure as Administrator has left a lasting and positive impression on America Samoa.

As a Pacific Islands Territory with its own geographical, social, and environmental challenges, environmental protection can be a difficult area of governance where programs spend much of their time and energy articulating the circumstances of our homeland. However, you demonstrated a genuine desire to understand and help America Samoa so that we may succeed in our environmental programs and services. For these reasons, I would like to express a heartfelt thanks and gratitude to you for fostering positive and effective inter-governmental relations.

In the truest sense, you have given American Samoa and the Pacific jurisdictions an elevated voice in the complex conversations surrounding environmental protection. That will be a legacy that will remain with the people of American Samoa and the Pacific well beyond your tenure.

I was so appreciative of the letter the governor sent me. I received similar messages from the people I came to know from the tribal lands and Pacific Island territories, and while my wife and I were so appreciative of this outreach, which helped me through some very depressing times, it was quite sad that so many people reached out to thank me for doing so much more than others ever had.

It is really sad that they all think I have done so much more when I did no more than what any regional administrator should do. It is really sad that by just giving them the respect, attention, and voice they deserve, they would be so grateful. Again, I gave them nothing more and nothing less than what they deserved and were entitled to.

Hopefully, going forward, giving tribes and territories what they deserve will not reap special accolades. Hopefully, giving them what they deserve will not be the exception but will become the norm. Why there is this willingness for neglect, I can't tell you, but I have my theories.

Why do our federal agencies neglect the Pacific Island territories? The most positive narrative would be to blame it on distance. They are located what most Americans don't even consider the United States of America. As previously noted in my discussion regarding the response to Super Typhoon Yutu in CNMI, even people in the EPA weren't even aware that a place called the Northern Mariana Islands was the USA and subject to the same federal environmental laws as our states.

When a hurricane devastated Puerto Rico, it was national news. But when Super Typhoon Yutu devastated CNMI, you didn't know a thing. There was no CNN, Fox, CBS, ABC, or NBC coverage simply because the Pacific Island territories are out of sight and out of mind. Very few United States citizens, with the exception of Pacific Island territory residents; meteorologists; and employees of the armed forces, especially the coast guard, the navy, and the Army Corps of Engineers; FEMA; EPA; NOAA; and the Department of the Interior ever even realized that the most powerful typhoon in US history devastated CNMI in November 2018. That fact is a very, very sad commentary.

I can't tell you how many times so many people have asked me why I go to Guam, American Samoa, and CNMI as part of my job with EPA, and I would respond by saying that because they are the United States and are within the jurisdiction of Region 9 of the US EPA. The response almost always got a blank stare on their face. I even had a conversation with a high-level presidential appointee in the EPA, who will remain nameless, who asked me why the EPA was doing anything in Saipan. They received the same response from me—because it is the United States and within the jurisdiction of Region 9 of the US EPA. And there was the same blank look on that person's face from what I said. Very sad.

In any event, I really think there is a failure in giving the Pacific Island territories a seat at the table when they are entitled to it or giving them the respect they have earned. These are all things I hope all federal agencies will be much more sensitive to going forward. As for our tribes, it is more troublesome. There is no excuse for distance. Our tribes are our Native Americans, who were here long before the rest of us or our ancestors. And on top of that, there are the legal requirements to treat tribes with respect, to treat them as sovereign nations, and to require government-to-government relations.

The United States has a unique legal and political relationship with Indian tribes and a special relationship with native Alaskan entities as provided in the Constitution of the United States, our treaties, and our federal statutes. These relationships extend to the federal government's historic preservation activities, mandating that federal consultation with Native American tribes be meaningful, in good faith, and entered into on a government-to-government basis.

On September 23, 2004, President George W. Bush issued the executive memorandum for government-to-government relationship with tribal governments, recommitting the federal government to work with federally recognized Native American tribal governments on a government-to-government basis and strongly supporting and respecting tribal sovereignty and self-determination. Mandates for the federal government's unique policies and relationship with Native American tribal governments are also codified in several executive orders.

- Executive Order 13007, "Indian Sacred Sites," was issued by President Clinton in 1996. It directed federal agencies to accommodate access to and ceremonial use of Native American sacred sites by Native American religious practitioners and to avoid adversely affecting the physical integrity of such sacred sites.
- Executive Order 13175, "Consultation and Coordination with Indian Tribal Governments," was issued by President Clinton in 2000. It recognized tribal rights of self-government and tribal sovereignty and affirmed and committed

the federal government to work with Native American tribal governments on a government-to-government basis.

I could provide numerous examples of this disconnect between our federal agencies and our tribes. However, I will just focus on one example: EPA GAP guidance. GAP stands for General Assistance Program. The EPA GAP program's goal is to assist tribes in developing the capacity to plan and establish environmental protection programs and to develop and implement solid and hazardous waste programs with their individual needs. In 2019, a total of $63,343,000 was allocated to our nation's tribes pursuant to GAP.

Several years ago, the inspector general (IG) issued a report that concluded that there was no appropriate oversight by EPA to the tribes to assure the GAP funds allocated were spent appropriately. In response to the IG report, the EPA implemented GAP funding guidelines that put a major burden on the tribes in regard to their GAP funding applications and their oversight of the funding to assure no misappropriations. In 2018, the EPA started a process to reassess those guidelines.

I learned within weeks on the job that the tribes had major problems with those revised guidelines. The end result was to cause tribes to spend so much more administrative time with the GAP funding. As a consequence, much more of the GAP funding requests covered administrative costs to monitor the program, and significantly fewer dollars were going out to fund actual environmental programs.

I thought that as a Republican political appointee, this would be a no-brainer. I immediately started advocating at the HQ level for revisions to the GAP guidelines. (I wish I could provide the letter I provided to HQ within two months of being sworn in, but as discussed previously, the EPA took all my personal files upon my termination.) In any event, my position with HQ was simple. We're Republicans. We believe in efficiency. We believe in getting unnecessary government out of the way. And we believe government funding should go to solving the problem, not to the administration of dealing with the problem.

Within a month of taking office, I advocated that our GAP guidance rules should be changed. The accounting issues that led to the earlier change in policy could be solved by the regional EPA office being responsible for more closely overseeing the funding that had been provided pursuant to a GAP grant. We could reverse the administrative hoops that had been created for our nation's tribes so that significantly more GAP dollars could go to real environmental programs and less into administrative oversight.

Within months, the EPA started a review of the GAP guidance rules. They started that review in November of 2018. The tribes were universally behind the changes that I advocated for. The rules went out for comment. Thousands of comments were received. I interfaced with HQ, and all I got was a bunch of legal mumbo jumbo why the guidance could not be changed in light of the IG report that caused the changes in the first place.

I consulted with my R9 attorneys and universally received the opinion that the decision could absolutely be changed. It could be changed without even going out for comment. This was not rulemaking. This was guidance that can be changed with a stroke of a pen overnight. Given the legal duty to consult with the tribes, at most, a consultation with them is required.

What we had was a policy call on whether GAP guidance that the tribes wanted to be changed should be changed. I provided a simple solution that would have satisfied the IG's concerns for accountability and the tribes' concern to spend more money on environmental protection and less on administrative burdensome oversight by putting the burden on the EPA to more closely monitor GAP funding. If we were really listening to the tribes, really trying to help them where they needed help, really pursuing policies that were consistent with the mission of the EPA, and really delivering to our tribal lands, this was an easy fix.

I am sorry to report that as of my writing this book, nothing has changed. This easy fix got caught up in the swamp, where things are not easy to change. EPA made changes in GAP guidance to respond to the IG. The IG was happy with the changes, as their only concern was accountability. Their concern was legitimate, and the tribes and

I had proposed a simple solution that would have solved the problem and free up literally millions of dollars that could have been spent on real-world environmental protection and not administrative oversight.

But it wouldn't happen because the EPA at the HQ level just didn't really listen to our nation's tribes. So much for Republicans running the government more efficiently, getting unnecessary government out of the way, and saving taxpayer money or assuring taxpayer money was spent on real projects versus administrative paperwork. For the sake of not wasting taxpayer money and for getting more dollars to our tribes for real environmental protection, I hope the EPA, with the new administration, will seriously reconsider the GAP guidance rules and adopt what our tribe's and I had proposed.

I provide this background as it is my opinion that the federal agencies do not take recognition of tribal sovereignty or government-to-government relationship anywhere as seriously as they should. That was my perspective of Trump's EPA, and that was what I observed of all federal agencies with the exception of FEMA. (It is in FEMA's DNA that they go wherever their mission assignment takes them. FEMA knows no boundaries. Distance doesn't matter. Whether the response and recovery are in tribal lands, the territories or a state doesn't matter for FEMA.)

If only all the federal agencies could respond in the same way. I don't believe this lack of respect is something new. I think it has been going on for a long time. Again, this is just my perspective, but it is what I truly believe based on what I observed while with the EPA and from my previous years of public service at the local, state, and federal level.

Going forward, I hope there will be a much more serious commitment given by all federal agencies to serve our tribes and Pacific Island territories. I will discuss in the chapter "Policy Recommendations for EPA Going Forward" what special programs and additional funding should be provided to serve our tribes and territories and, at the same time, better achieve EPA's goals in supporting environmental justice, promoting brownfield developments, and help our tribes and territories reach the same levels for environmental protections as the rest of the general public.

For instance, 91 percent of the US population has safe drinking water. In tribal lands, when I left the EPA, only 73 percent of the tribal populations has safe drinking water. I strongly recommend to the US EPA that they make it a national priority that the percentage of safe drinking water on tribal lands equal the national percentage by the year 2025.

One thing I do know from my tenure as R9 RA is, I will be forever committed to doing whatever I can in whatever capacity I am serving to advocate for our nation's tribes and the Pacific Island territories. They are incredible people, and they deserve nothing less.

CHAPTER 8

Superfund and Emergency Management

THERE IS A REASON the Superfund and emergency management functions of EPA are both part of one division. Both involve some of the most challenging and stressful jobs EPA has to deal with.

Superfund

In the case of Superfund, EPA is currently responding to an environmental nightmare that is a by-product of actions taken years ago, when we didn't know better. DDT were emptied into rivers or storm drains that emptied into oceans. Manufacturers discharged toxins from their operations into the sewers or into the groundwater basin. Mining operations poured mercury, lead, copper, and other chemicals into our nation's rivers and, therefore, into the drinking supply. The list goes on and on.

The bottom line is that the Superfund division is there to right the environmental wrongs of our past. It is there to take over whatever horrible environmental legacy was left over and remediate it and restore a horrible environmental outcome to a situation that is contained and is finally being managed.

The law that gives rise to the EPA listing a site on the Superfund National Priority List (NPL) is CERCLA, or the Comprehensive Environmental Response, Compensation, and Liability Act, which was enacted by Congress on December 11, 1980.

> The Comprehensive Environmental Response, Compensation, and Liability Act (CERCLA), commonly known as Superfund, was enacted by Congress on December 11, 1980. This law created a tax on the chemical and petroleum industries and provided broad Federal authority to respond directly to releases or threatened releases of hazardous substances that may endanger human health or the environment. Over five years, $1.6 billion was collected and the tax went to a trust fund for cleaning up abandoned or uncontrolled hazardous waste sites. The Comprehensive Environmental Response, Compensation, and Liability Act of 1980 (CERCLA):
>
> - established prohibitions and requirements concerning closed and abandoned hazardous waste sites;
> - provided for liability of persons responsible for releases of hazardous waste at these sites; and
> - established a trust fund to provide for cleanup when no responsible party could be identified.

Previously, I discussed Superfund NPL sites at Casmalia, Hunters Point, Montrose, Copper Mountain, and Iron Mountain. When I left the EPA, I would have added to that list Tronox (Vegas), the San Gabriel Valley, the San Fernando Valley, Halaco, Pearl Harbor, Factory Street in Honolulu, and what I consider the biggest challenge the US EPA faces, the Navajo abandoned uranium mines (AUM).

I spent the week of April 14, 2019, touring Navajo Nation. I met with the president of Navajo Nation, President Jonathan Nez, and the directors of Navajo Nation EPA and Navajo Nation Superfund. On my first day in Navajo Nation, I delivered opening remarks at a job fair that was being sponsored by R9's EPA. This was an important event, as EPA would be awarding the first contracts toward AUM Superfund remediation. Those contracts would total $220 million.

As mentioned previously, the Tronox trust fund to be used exclusively for Superfund remediation for the AUMs was almost $1.8 billion. More on this trust fund and the private sector contractors who will do the remediation work later. For now, let me focus on the extent of the problem with the AUMs.

For the remainder of that week, I would tour many of the AUMs. My staff, myself, and Navajo Nation Superfund director Dariel Yazzie would put 1,200 miles on our car, starting in Albuquerque and ending in Flagstaff. I only saw a glimpse of the scope of the AUM issue in the 1,200 miles I covered. That is how big the Navajo Nation is. Navajo Nation is basically the size of West Virginia. That is the reason I advocated with HQ to support listing Navajo Nation as an EPA geographical program to join the Gulf of Mexico, the Great Lakes, and the Chesapeake Bay.

By being one of the designated substantial geographical programs, significant additional revenues are appropriated annually to meet the needs of that program. The three other substantial geographical programs—the Gulf of Mexico, the Great Lakes, and the Chesapeake Bay—also come with their own geographic office. Consequently, the designation of Navajo Nation as a substantial geographic program would also bring a much-deserved Region 9 field office for the nation, something I also lobbied HQ for while I was the RA. Navajo Nation deserves to be the next substantial geographical program designated by EPA with their own field office.

In an NPR human health report on April 10, 2016, entitled "For the Navajo Nation, Uranium Mining's Deadly Legacy Lingers," the report stated the following:

> The federal government is cleaning up a long legacy of uranium mining within the Navajo Nation—some 27,000 square miles spread across Utah, New Mexico and Arizona that is home to more than 250,000 people. Many Navajo people have died of kidney failure and cancer, conditions linked to uranium contamination. And new research for the CDC shows uranium in babies born now. Mining companies blasted 4 million tons of uranium out of Navajo land between 1944 and 1986. The federal government purchased the ore to make atomic weapons. As the Cold war threat petered out the companies left, abandoning more than 500 mines.
>
> Maria Welch is a field researcher with the Southwest Research Information Center, which is working with the federal CDC... One of the study's findings: 27% of the participants have high level of uranium in their urine, compared to 5% of the U.S. population as a whole... Many Navajo unwittingly let their livestock drink for those [uranium contaminated] pools, and their children play in mine debris piles. Some even built their homes out of uranium... Why isn't there more of an outrage? [Ms. Welch] asks.

Well, the EPA is finally doing something about it, but Ms. Welch is absolutely correct in asking why there is not more of an outrage outside of the Navajo Nation. The resources R9 were given was enough to allocate a small team of, as I remember, five career staff full-time equivalents (FTEs) to be on the Navajo Nation AUM project team. These folks in EPA lingo are referred to as remedial project managers (RPMs). RPMs comprise the management team who works for the Superfund manager, who is the key person responsible for managing the Superfund site.

In the case of Navajo Nation's abandoned uranium mines, that manager is Will Duncan, who is also the assistant director of the R9 Superfund division. Will and his RPMs did an incredible job with the limited resources they had to work with. One person can only do so much, and the scope of the AUM problem in the Navajo Nation is huge. The lack of headquarters allocating the necessary amount of RPMs led the inspector general to issue a report identifying the magnitude of the problem and harshly criticized the EPA for their misallocation of RPMs in the Superfund divisions in the region with special emphasis put on the lack of RPMs allocated to Region 9.[9]

As a result of my lobbying HQ, they finally agreed to a novel and first time use of Superfund trust fund money that would lead to the allocation of an additional five RPMs exclusively to Navajo Nation's AUM project team. As previously mentioned, Superfund trust fund money must be legally spent solely on the Superfund site for which the trust fund is established for.

Given that legal requirement, I advocated to HQ to allow R9 to hire new RPMs in the R9 Superfund division who would be used exclusively on the Navajo Nation AUM project. Previously, trust fund money had never been used to hire RPMs as EPA employees, but the Navajo Nation supported this use of the Tronox trust fund established for the Navajo Nation AUMs. Ultimately, HQ agreed; and from everything I know, those individuals have now been hired, which essentially doubles the number of the R9 EPA career staff working on the AUM project.

Based on what my staff demonstrated to the HQ staff, those additional RPMs, or full-time equivalents (FTEs), will significantly shorten the timetable for remediating the AUMs. Notwithstanding that improvement, I join Ms. Welch in asking, why isn't there more

---

9   IG report regarding superfund employee distribution problems within EPA: https://www.epa.gov/sites/production/files/2017-09/documents/_epaoig_ 20170919-17-p-0397_glance.pdf.

outrage? Unfortunately, notwithstanding the inspector general's report referenced above, Administrator Wheeler failed to address the lack of FTEs allocated to R9 for Superfund work. He punted and chose to leave it up to the Biden administration to address. Hopefully, they will.

If you're reading this, Congressman O'Halleran, I urge you to strongly impress upon Administrator Regan that FTEs working in the Superfund and Emergency Management Division within the regions should be reallocated. EPA's own internal assessment demonstrates that it is needed and warranted. I can assure you, the Navajo Nation will benefit greatly with this reallocation.

Congressman Tom O'Halleran, who represents the vast majority of Navajo Nation, has been relentless in advocating for the Navajo Nation and for the federal government to address the AUMs issue. Having watched him in action and having had the pleasure of working with him on Navajo Nation issues, I have the greatest respect and admiration for him. Former congresswoman Deb Haaland, who represents a much smaller portion of Navajo Nation, has also been a true champion for the people of Navajo Nation, but they have not been given support by their colleagues in Congress.

The good news for our tribal lands, our Native Americans, and especially, Navajo Nation is, Congresswoman Haaland was appointed by President Biden as the secretary of the interior. In March 2021, she was confirmed by the US Senate. She became the first Native American presidential cabinet secretary. I take comfort in knowing our country's Native Americans have a strong advocate in President Biden's administration.

The time has come for EPA to add Navajo Nation as the next geographical program, which will mean much greater federal funding for Navajo Nation and for cleanup of the AUMs. Designating Navajo Nation as the next geographical program will also elevate the challenges Navajo Nation faces regarding the AUMs with Congress. Elevating the issue at the congressional level by acknowledging Navajo Nation as a geographical program will also assist congressional members O'Halleran's and Haaland's future successors in their advocacy efforts with their colleagues regarding Navajo Nation.

EPA should take this action, as the Navajo Nation meets all the criteria for a geographical program, and EPA should do it because this problem was created and inflicted upon the people of Navajo Nation for mining uranium to go into our atomic weapons. The people of Navajo Nation, their land, their farms, their rivers, and their streams have been contaminated by uranium to provide for our country's defense.

It is time for the EPA to publicly acknowledge that this country owes the people of Navajo Nation more. It is time for the EPA to declare Navajo Nation a geographical program. If you are reading this, Congressman O'Halleran and Secretary Haaland, please urge EPA administrator Regan to designate Navajo Nation as EPA's next substantial geographic program with a geographic office.

Here's one final observation regarding the AUMs Superfund remediation going forward. I mentioned that my first day in Navajo Nation started with the Navajo Nation AUMs jobs fair. There is one thing EPA should commit to in the future with regard to AUM remediation contracts in the private sector. All efforts should be taken to assure that as many Navajo Nation businesses as possible get AUM remediation contracts.

As the prime contractor in many cases is going to have prerequisites that most Navajo Nation businesses will not be able to qualify for, EPA needs to change the rules for the use of subcontractors to assure that all qualified Navajo Nation subcontractors are used by the prime contractors who are awarded the contracts. The scoring for the award of the contracts should be changed so that listing of Navajo Nation businesses as subcontractors in the prime contract will score much higher than the current rules provide for. This will give a huge incentive for the prime contractor to search out as many qualified Navajo Nation subcontractors to be listed in the bid.

I am not advocating that nonqualified contractors ever be used. I am just saying that if the prime contractor is given a much greater incentive to find Navajo Nation subcontractors, they will find subs who most likely will not be identified or listed under the current guidance. Again, it is the Navajo Nation people who have paid the price for our nation mining their mountains to provide for the defense of our country. Every effort should, therefore, be made so that Navajo Nation businesses are given contracts as part of the AUM Superfund remediation process that will be taking place for decades to come.

Between my discussion regarding the EPA Superfund program in this chapter and in the chapter "The First 100 Days," I don't believe there is much of a need to go into the details of Tronox (Vegas), Pearl Harbor, Halaco, the San Gabriel Valley, the San Fernando Valley, or Factory Street, which were the Superfund sites that I visited after my first one hundred days. These are all incredible engineering marvels where the EPA is doing the job that they always do at any Superfund site, and that is providing the remediation necessary to protect human health and the environment. I will leave you with something I mentioned to my staff while visiting either Tronox (Vegas) or the San Gabriel Valley sites.

I've already discussed the personal connection I had with Casmalia for being the Santa Barbara County supervisor, for taking the initiative to have Casmalia listed on the EPA Superfund NPL, and then for being the R9 administrator who signed the Record of Decision to start the process to remove Casmalia from the NPL. And then there was Tronox (Vegas) and the San Gabriel Valley Superfund sites.

Tronox (Vegas) had manufacturing taking place from the fifties through the eighties. Their operations caused chemicals to go into the groundwater basin. That basin essentially drained underground to the Colorado River. The San Gabriel Valley Superfund site—there are actually six areas within the 170-square-mile San Gabriel Valley— much like the Orange County North Basin, which was listed on the NPL after I departed EPA, had numerous manufacturing companies that during the fifties through the seventies disposed of volatile organic compounds (VOCs) and industrial solvents.

So what was my personal connection to these sites? My parents had a second house on the Colorado River in Parker, Arizona. We had that house from 1962 until 1972. I would stay there almost all summer long and many of the weekends during the spring and fall. The water we drank came from pumping water out of the river. That water would be determined decades later to be contaminated with the chemicals that had been discharged by Tronox (Vegas) upstream.

From 1959 through 1963, we lived in La Puente before moving to Arcadia. We lived near the first In-N-Out Burger that opened up in the late fifties. That In-N-Out-Burger establishment was at the center of what would be the San Gabriel Valley Superfund site decades later. We drank our water out of the tap. Water that was coming from the toxic, contaminated groundwater that the San Gabriel Valley Superfund site would start remediating in the mid 1980s, twenty years after I drank water out of the tap. So essentially, from 1959 through 1972, I was drinking my water from what would become EPA Superfund NPL sites for groundwater contamination.

Before leaving the topic of Superfund, I would be remiss if I don't mention a couple of my former staff who make that division work so well with the limited resources they are provided. As previously discussed by EPA's own internal FTE allocation assessments, R9 was sixty-plus FTEs short in the Superfund and Emergency Management Division.

Since the inception of the EPA, however, R9 has been significantly shorted when it comes to FTE allocations for Superfund and emergency management. The man who is the current division director for R9 is Enrique Manzanilla. He has addressed so much with limited resources. He deserves great credit.

I had my doubts about Enrique in the beginning. My doubts were from my first encounter with him when we dealt with the challenges while in Hawaii with the volcano. (Remember my earlier discussion about how he pushed back on me wanting to have the state of Hawaii make a mission assignment request with FEMA.)

Those doubts were quickly eliminated. By the time we spent a week together in Navajo Nation on the road, he had my full confidence. By Navajo Nation, I knew how lucky R9 was to have Enrique as the Superfund and Emergency Management Division director.

And then there was Enrique's deputy, John Lyon's. John and I hit it off on day one. We had something very much in common. Our commonality had nothing to do with the environment, and it had nothing to do with our backgrounds or our education. It had only one thing to do with, and that was that we were both Deadheads. As all Deadheads know, there is a common bond that brings us together. John, let me dedicate "New Speedway Boogie" to you.

And then in addition to Will Duncan managing Navajo Nation AUM, there were Superfund managers Angeles Herrera and Dana Barton. I worked closely with both Angeles and Dana in regard to several other Region 9 Superfund sites. These managers are two of the most important persons involved with a Superfund NPL site. They are the intermediary between EPA, the concerned public, the stakeholders, and the private sector contractors.

I worked with Angeles on Hunters Point and Pearl Harbor. I worked with Will on Navajo Nation. I worked with Dana on Montrose and San Gabriel Valley. Angeles, Will, and Dana have my greatest respect. They have all done an exemplary job in dealing with some very controversial situations. They are dedicated, and they are professional. They are the best of the best in the world of Superfund. And then there are the best of the best in the world of emergency management.

Emergency Management

As for emergency management, EPA is often the second most active federal agency behind FEMA in responding to federally declared emergencies. Whether it is fires, floods, hurricanes, tornados, or typhoons, when Mother Nature has finished inflicting her toll from the event, EPA is there to clean up the waters, clean up the hazardous household waste, and locate and prepare for the disposal of asbestos-laden transformers that have fallen to the ground. The list goes on and on.

Significantly, the men and women career staff of EPA who work in the emergency management division are often deployed out of their regions, often stay there for weeks, are without their families during deployment, whether that means Christmas, as was the case in R9 with the Camp Fire in Paradise or Super Typhoon Yutu in Saipan in 2018, and are the ones who restore some sense of hope for a community to move forward and get their lives back together again.

By now, you know how much praise I have for all the career men and women who work for the US EPA. They are all truly the most passionate, dedicated, and professional people I have ever worked with. However, the career staff in emergency management quickly became the staff I have the greatest respect for as a result of the sacrifices they have made, as mentioned briefly above. Consequently, emergency management, which I had not initially focused on as a personal RA priority, quickly became one of my highest priorities.

In the chapter "The First 100 Days," I discussed the EPA's emergency management to the Hawaii volcano, and I mentioned I met Steve Calanog in Hawaii for the first time. Steve was the on-scene coordinator. When we met with his team and the Coast Guard Strike Team, I could sense from his body language that he had his doubts about this rookie RA, who was recently appointed by President Trump. He was respectful, but I know when someone is not a fan of me. On that morning, Steve was definitely not a fan.

I would see Steve from time to time in R9's San Francisco office over the next seven months. The next time I would see Steve on-site as the on-scene coordinator would be in Chico for the Camp Fire the following December. More on that emergency management to follow.

What I think is important to point out is that between Hawaii and Chico, Steve saw firsthand my commitment to the emergency management team. He saw that I would be a strong advocate at the HQ level for their needs and wants as well. He saw that I was all in and that I not only talked the talk but walked the walk.

By Chico, Steve and I had developed an incredible bond. I have no idea where I rank in Steve's mind in relation to the other R9 RAs with whom he has worked, but I do know what he sent me immediately after my termination. On February 7, 2020, three days after being fired, Steve emailed me the following:

Mike,

I was on travel for work this week in Philadelphia when I received news of your departure. I was shocked and saddened. You have been a tremendous supporter of the work that we do in the Emergency Management Program during your tenure. Our work does transcend politics! You recognized that the first day we met in Hawaii when you came out during the volcano response.

Your enthusiasm and pride in our work was and is infectious. You have championed ER work regionally and nationally. I really appreciate that and thank you profoundly! Best wishes and good luck. I hope our cross paths again soon under better circumstances.

Steve, I hope they cross as well. You are the real deal, and it would be my honor to work with you in any capacity. In 2019, Steve was named the EPA on-scene coordinator of the year. All our on-scene coordinators are incredible people who deal with very stressful situations and make incredible sacrifices in their personal lives. They all deserve to be recognized for the job they do, but someone was going to be the EPA's on-scene coordinator of the year, and there was no one more deserving from my perspective than Steve Calanog.

As I mentioned above, the next time I met Steve was in Chico for the morning briefing at the incident command center (ICC) for the Camp Fire. The emergency management for the Camp Fire was a national response, meaning emergency responders were being deployed from all ten regions to assist with the R9 team. As I recall, there were twenty-seven people who were introduced, going around the room to start the morning briefing. I can't even start to convey the emotional feeling I had as people were making their introductions.

Of the twenty-seven people, I believe only three, including Steve, were from R9. All twenty-four other people were emergency responders from the other nine regions. These were career EPA emergency management staff from all over the country. These were committed emergency responders who had left their homes and their families during Christmas to be deployed for two to three weeks to respond to the Camp Fire. I can't even begin to describe the extent of my respect and admiration for what they do.

After the briefing, we toured the town of Paradise. Paradise had essentially been totally destroyed by the fire. It was a town one day and nothing the next. The EPA was there to carry out our FEMA mission statement to remove downed telephone transformers and all hazardous household waste. Literally, our responders went lot to lot to remove hazardous house waste from the properties. Until they painted a green on a marker on each lot, the property was not considered clean. Once painted green, EPA's job for that parcel was complete. Keeping in mind that almost every structure burned down, our folks needed to essentially clear every lot that existed in the town of Paradise.

Our team opened the incident command center in early December 2018. I advised Administrator Wheeler that based on the FEMA mission assignment, our work could potentially continue until May or June of 2019. That was based on the information my staff provided me based on their assessment from past experiences. FEMA agreed with our assessment.

In an incredible testimonial to Steve and his colleagues, R9 completed our FEMA mission assignment in just over 60 days. FEMA's Region 9 administrator, Bob Fenton, would publicly state in March 2019 that the R9 emergency management to the Camp Fire was unprecedented in his years of experience with FEMA. He had never seen any federal agency respond so well to their FEMA mission assignment. He was spot-on. Our team did in just over 60 days what everyone felt at the outset would easily take 180 days.

There is only one good thing that comes out of a disaster. Your emergency responders learn and are that much faster and efficient the next time a disaster comes along. In the case of the Camp Fire, my folks had learned from the emergency management to the Napa and Sonoma fires in October 2017. From that disaster and response, they implemented what they learned two years later with the Camp Fire, and their response speaks for itself, an incredible achievement by any account.

Before and after my touring of the Camp Fire, I went to the Northern Mariana Islands (CNMI) to respond to Super Typhoon Yutu. As mentioned in the earlier chapter, "The Tribes and the Pacific Island Territories," the typhoon was devastating in terms of the damage she reaped. That emergency management was also a national response.

On Tinian, the on-scene coordinator was from Region 2, Philadelphia. His name was Keith Glenn. When we met, we immediately hit it off. Unlike my first encounter with Steve during my second week on the job, when Steve had his initial doubts, now seven months later, word had gotten out nationwide that the R9 administrator was the real thing when it came to supporting the mission of emergency responders. Two weeks after I was terminated, Keith emailed me.

> Hi, Mike. I had the pleasure of meeting and working with you during Super Typhoon Yutu, on Tinian. I wanted to let you know that the experience I had on that response was personally rewarding. I learned an incredible amount regarding the history of our great country, what it meant to work with the Chamorro people and the unique complexities of the area. I have to say that it was a pleasure to see you light up when we went to see the Seabees and got to pay homage to your grandfather. That was very humbling and a story that I continue to tell. I will always remember the story of your grandfather's ring and how you were able to bring it back to Tinian under different circumstances than when it was forged.
>
> I wanted to let you know that many of the OSCs (On-Scene Coordinator), even those of us on the east coast, remember your spirit, leadership and championing of our program and our agency. I don't know the circumstances surrounding your departure from the agency; however,

you should know that it has been a significant loss to us as individuals and professionals.

Your credibility remains with us. Your passion remains with us. Your legacy remains with us. While I have been deployed to places and situations all over the country during my 22-year tenure, meeting and working beside you was a rewarding and memorable highlight. I wish you all the best and hope our paths will cross again. Stay safe and stay well my friend.

Keith, you don't know how much I also hope our paths cross again, and I strongly feel that will indeed happen. Before leaving the subject matter of emergency responders, I would be neglectful if I don't point out a fact that seems to get little attention at the HQ level. I've discussed the FTE allocation shortfall for R9 in the Superfund and Emergency Management Division. By November 2018, most of the emergency responders and OSCs had maxed out on how much they could work, meaning future deployments would essentially be pro bono.

The California fires and Super Typhoon Yutu hit with significant deployments needed. Although almost all the R9 emergency management staff and the OSCs were maxed out, they all, nonetheless, volunteered to deploy. That's the kind of people they are. That's the kind of employees this country has working for them in the world of EPA's emergency management. To all the emergency responders at the US EPA, I salute you. You are all the best of the best.

CHAPTER 9

Fema and Resiliency

While this book is intended to let the reader understand what the EPA and its career staff are really all about, I welcome the opportunity with this book to highlight the wonderful work that is done by FEMA. When there is a federally declared emergency, FEMA goes to work and issues mission assignments (MAs) to all the other federal agencies. Based on the mission assignment, any federal agency may play a role. However, be assured that the EPA, the Coast Guard, and the Army Corps of Engineers are almost always involved. And in most cases, for the reasons previously stated, it is not uncommon for the EPA to be the second most active federal agency involved in the disaster and in the fulfillment of the FEMA mission assignment.

As a result of the EPA's role in emergencies, the EPA and FEMA have developed a very close, cordial working relationship. That is definitely the case with R9 for EPA and FEMA. My FEMA counterpart, Bob Fenton, and I had a very good, close working relationship. FEMA was lucky to have Bob.

One of the accomplishments I am very proud of is R9 EPA's work with R9 FEMA during the recovery stage of Super Typhoon Yutu. I previously mentioned my interface with R9 deputy RA Bill Roche when establishing a recovery project list. At the end of the day, we were successful in our recovery project list being supported by FEMA. And as a consequence, almost $65 million was appropri-

197

ated from Congress to CNMI for their recovery efforts. I say that was unprecedented as the money that was allocated, prior to Super Typhoon Yutu, would never have been appropriated pursuant to the traditional FEMA guidance for recovery projects.

Working with FEMA, we strongly pushed resiliency in justifying recovery projects that would not have been supported prior to the CNMI typhoon, and it is due to the concept of resiliency why I wanted to write this chapter. I believe the issue of resiliency will be a huge factor for all communities devastated by disasters in the future. They will be able to receive that much more federal recovery dollars in the future.

I previously mentioned the road map John McCarroll and I implemented to be successful in our advocacy with FEMA for approval of recovery projects. John deserves so much credit for what was ultimately appropriated to CNMI in recovery disaster funds. He had the initial idea. He sold me on it while I was on the ground in Saipan. We both agreed we needed to do two things to get FEMA to support a new approach for recoveries in disasters.

We had to convince FEMA that it made sense to spend more to create resiliency so that less will be destroyed in future disasters, and therefore, less costs will be incurred to the federal government in future disasters. And we had to convince CNMI that they had to seriously embrace resiliency and that if they did, the payoff would be a much greater recovery appropriation from Congress. Fortunately, thanks to John's creative thinking and my aggressive advocacy, our strategy paid off.

In CNMI, they were operating under the 2002 International Building Code (IBC). That code was very much outdated. I met with Congressman Sablan, CNMI state legislators Tina Sablan and Ed Probst, and CNMI Office of Planning and Development (OPM) representatives Kodep Ogumoro-Uludong and Elizabeth Balajadia. I told them that the best way I could be successful in my lobbying FEMA would be if I could assure FEMA that CNMI was going to be very serious about resiliency, their building codes, and their building inspectors going forward.

I wanted to be able to make a case that if FEMA would do more for CNMI in recovery, CNMI would do more to assure their building structures would be more resilient to withstand future storms. To accomplish that, CNMI needed to commit to changes going forward.

First, the state legislature needed to adopt the more stringent 2018 IBC. Second, CNMI needed to commit to assuring their building inspectors would be better trained and would be knowledgeable of the building codes they were enforcing. (It was well known that the building inspectors in CNMI were not very well trained and, in many cases, were high school graduates who had very little knowledge of the building codes they were enforcing.) My argument was that building codes, even the 2018 IBCs, mean very little if the inspectors enforcing those codes don't have the experience or knowledge to understand those codes.

I received full assurances from the representatives in CNMI that they would support these changes. In 2019, the state legislature passed legislation adopting the 2018 IBC, and the governor signed it into law. As for the training of building inspectors, John and I put together a proposal where FEMA would provide funding for a two-year program to bring in experts to train the CNMI building inspectors, at which time CNMI would be responsible going forward for only employing well-qualified, well-trained building inspectors who know and understand and know how to enforce the 2018 IBCs. CNMI also fully supported this proposal.

When I returned on my second trip to CNMI in January 2019, I was able to discuss our R9 recovery project list with Bill Roche. More importantly, I was able to represent to Bill that in considering our list, it should be assessed with the understanding that CNMI wanted to show how serious they were with FEMA to create a more resilient CNMI. They would be pursuing legislation to adopt the 2018 IBC, and then I proposed the two-year FEMA role with regard to CNMI's building inspectors.

Bill was elated about the possibility of the 2018 IBC being adopted. We both agreed that would be huge in future disasters, and furthermore, we both agreed a much more resilient building code wouldn't mean anything if the building inspectors didn't really know what to inspect for and were just inclined to sign off on building permits.

Consequently, Bill said he was very interested in the two-year building inspector program I proposed. Ultimately, Bill and FEMA would support that program. Unfortunately, that program was not funded in the congressional recovery appropriation bill. Hopefully, Congressman Sablan, with the help of his colleagues in the Congress, will be able to get this program funded in future appropriation bills, perhaps infrastructure legislation.

The good news was, John and my advocacy of one word—*resiliency*—was a game changer. The resiliency mindset in CNMI was fundamentally changed thanks to the support of the 2018 IBC by the legislature and the governor from the outset. John and I created a dialogue that focused on the need for a better building code and better building inspectors to assure that code was enforced. We started a dialogue that got everyone on the same page: if CNMI would take their building codes and resiliency seriously, FEMA would be able to do more, and the end result would be that many more buildings would be left standing in future disasters.

Thank you, Bill Roche. Thank you, Bob Fenton. Thank you, FEMA. And thank you, Governor Torres, Congressman Sablan, and state legislators Sablan and Probst. Your leadership made a huge difference, and CNMI will be that much more resilient for it in the years to come.

And, Bob, what a pleasure it was to meet you halfway between Chico and San Francisco, in front of that Subway sandwich shop, to give you the recovery project list John and his team put together with the help of Juliette Hayes from FEMA. Without Juliette's help, we would never have been successful in our advocacy efforts for CNMI. She was instrumental in putting together a recovery list that FEMA would consider credible.

As for the list, I promised Bill on my first trip to CNMI in December 2018 that I would get the list to Bob in mid-January 2019. The R9 crew had just finished the list, and I wanted to personally deliver it to Bob. Bob had been up in Paradise with FEMA, dealing with the Camp Fire, and was driving back to the R9 FEMA HQ in

Oakland. I was in the R9 EPA HQ in San Francisco and would be driving up to Chico to be with my R9 EPA emergency responders and tour Paradise the next day.

We both agreed that the easiest way to get the list personally to him was to meet halfway, as we would be passing each other on Interstate 80. We met, Bob got the list, and several months later, CNMI got $65 million. Recovery mission for CNMI was accomplished all in the name of resiliency!

CHAPTER 10

Transboundary Sewage at the US-Mexico Border

I PREVIOUSLY DISCUSSED MY advocacy for EPA to make addressing transboundary sewage at the US-Mexico border a national priority, which Administrator Wheeler chose not to elevate. Ken Wagner, when he was still with the agency, was a huge advocate, as was the assistant administrator for the Office of Water, David Ross. For that, I can't thank them both enough.

With Administrator Wheeler choosing not to make the issue an EPA priority, I continued to meet with the stakeholders in Arizona and California. The closest I ever came to being reprimanded for anything I did as the R9 RA was when Administrator Wheeler called me to lambast me for outreach regarding the transboundary sewage issue.

In a meeting Administrator Wheeler evidently had with Speaker Pelosi, the speaker referenced the information I provided her summarizing the costs necessary to address the transboundary sewage issue. That cost estimate had been put together by R9 and R6 as a very preliminary assessment. That assessment was a document available to anyone in the public who wanted it. That cost was just over $350 million.

For providing the speaker that information, which I provided to all the stakeholders, the administrator wrongfully concluded I had been lobbying Congress. Had I been lobbying Congress, that would have been an ethical violation, as EPA employees cannot lobby Congress for or against anything. I assured him I would never cross the line in lobbying for anything with Congress, and I never did.

But I did educate members of Congress on the issue and what it would take to solve the problem, and I continued to educate the stakeholders with all the facts I had to arm them with the ammunition they needed in their advocacy efforts. And there is nothing unethical about that. On the contrary, I think it is the responsibility of the EPA to provide interested members of the public all the non-privileged information the EPA has related to that issue.

But I strongly believe Wheeler felt differently. He was more than content for the status quo to be maintained with regard to the transboundary sewage issue. I truly believe his call and his warning to me was an attempt by him to intimidate me in hopes that I would stand down and back off my ethical outreach efforts. Well, those who know me know I don't intimidate easily. On the contrary, when someone attempts to intimidate me, I usually double down in my efforts. In the case of transboundary sewage, I was already 100 percent in, so doubling down wasn't a possibility.

So I continued my outreach. I reminded all the stakeholders in San Diego that I could not ethically lobby Congress but that they could, and lobby they did—Imperial mayor Dedina, Coronado mayor Bailey, San Diego mayor Faulconer, San Diego County supervisor Cox, board members from the San Diego port authority, and union representatives for the US Customs and Border Protection. The list goes on and on.

They did lobby, and thankfully, they were able to get the White House's attention. And in the end, in December 2019, in final negotiations with the White House over the US-Mexico trade agreement, Speaker Pelosi put on the table support for the agreement if the White House would add the $350 million appropriation to the US EPA to address the problem at the San Diego-Tijuana sector of the border. The White House agreed, the trade agreement passed, and now the issue will be finally addressed, at least in the San Diego-Tijuana sector.

What I'll never know is why Administrator Wheeler couldn't see that for a relatively small price tag, at least by federal standards, the Trump administration could have taken a huge victory lap on completely solving a major environmental disaster confronting this country. The vision I had was for President Trump and our administration to take 100 percent credit for solving the problem. I wanted our administration to acknowledge the problem and say it was time that the problem was resolved.

At the end of the day, President Trump and Speaker Pelosi both deserve credit. What could have been a win for team Trump, however, with regard to the environment, ended up just being a win for the environment. I blame Administrator Wheeler for not comprehending the issue and not taking the issue on as one that our administration would solve. The good news is, regardless of his shortsightedness, ultimately, as a result of my outreach and the advocacy of third-party stakeholders, the mission of the EPA to protect human health and the environment was served, and that's what matters.

The entire problem, however, has not been solved. The San Diego-Tijuana sector will be addressed because of the size of the bully pulpit of the stakeholders in that area, but my outreach and education had been to address the entire issue from Texas and the Gulf of Mexico to California and the Pacific Ocean. For California, the problem will be solved. However, for the remainder of the border, an environmental nightmare still exists, especially in Arizona, in Nogales, and in Naco.

From the assessments Regions 6 and 9 had done, the cost for addressing the problem for the remainder of the entire border would be less than the $350 million allocated to address just the problem at the San Diego-Tijuana sector. What the Trump administration could have taken as a huge environmental win was squandered. For the sake of those living in the border towns along the US-Mexico border in Arizona and Texas, I hope the Biden administration will see that opportunity and take the victory lap I would have preferred the Trump administration had run.

CHAPTER 11

Clean and Healthy Oceans

WHILE I BELIEVE THAT almost every division at HQ is overstaffed with FTEs at the expense of the regions being understaffed, the one exception is the Office of Wetlands, Oceans, and Watersheds (OWOW). The name speaks for itself. This is the staff that works on the issues pertaining to the nation's wetlands, our watersheds, and the ocean. From my recollection, I believe there are approximately one hundred people who work for this division in HQ.

From the national estuaries, to marine debris, to ocean microplastics, to wetlands protection, and to the protection of our coral reefs, these people do an amazing job, doing so much with so little. I personally believe that the new administrator, Administrator Regan, should take a serious look at this division and the role they want it to play regarding the ocean.

Historically, the focus of the EPA ended where the Waters of the US (WOTUS) ended. The Clean Water Act had a legal requirement for a nexus to the WOTUS. After the enactment of the Clean Water Act, the army corps and EPA, in their rulemaking, continually expanded the definition of what was considered a WOTUS. The courts went along with that expansion.

Finally, the US Supreme Court in *Rapanos v. the United States* (2006) ruled in favor of a more restrictive definition of what is considered navigable waters of the US. This led to more confusion, and the EPA in the Obama administration in 2015 attempted to adopt through the rulemaking process the previously more liberal definition of navigable waters. That rule was initially nationwide by a federal court of appeals.

In 2017, EPA announced its intent to review and rescind the rule (see "Intention to Review and Rescind or Revise the Clean Water Rule" [Notice 82 FR 12532. 2017-03-06]). A Supreme Court ruling on January 22, 2018, returned to the rule's nationwide authority. It gave back jurisdiction previously complicated by decisions from the circuit court of appeals. Two weeks later, the EPA suspended the rule and started their own rulemaking process. The proposed rule explicitly excluded twelve categories of waters that were previously covered by WOTUS. Some of those categories included the following:

1. groundwater, including groundwater drained through subsurface drainage systems
2. ephemeral streams and features that flow only in direct response to precipitation
3. ditches, including agricultural ditches, that are not traditional navigable waters and are not constructed in adjacent wetlands and do not relocate a tributary of traditional navigable waters
4. prior converted cropland
5. artificially irrigated areas that would revert to upland if artificial irrigation ceases

Significantly, when determining if a water body meets the jurisdictional definition, the federal agency shall consider the circumstances during a typical year. In other words, in a normal year's rainfall, the ephemeral stream would never run to the ocean to create the connection to navigable water. It henceforth would not be a navigable water and, therefore, not a WOTUS. On June 22, 2020, the EPA finalized the new rule.

Personally, I believe one of the greatest accomplishments of Trump's EPA was the adoption of this new rule, and I am proud of the role I was able to play in seeing that rule be adopted. There is no question in my mind that the final rule adopted in June 2020 is consistent with what Congress intended when they passed the Clean Water Act in 1972.

Keeping in mind that federal agencies' rulemaking powers are to be consistent with the original congressional intent of the legislation passed that gives rise to the rulemaking powers to adopt rules necessary to carry out the legislation, I believe Trump's EPA finally righted years of federal agencies, far exceeding what Congress originally intended. The Supreme Court in Rapanos seems to suggest that as well.

Here's one last comment regarding Trump's EPA redefining the definition of WOTUS to be consistent with the original intent of Congress when they passed the Clean Water Act. Those who argue that the redefining of WOTUS significantly weakens the efforts to clean the waterways in the US, I remind them that if the connection Congress required in the Clean Water Act exists, nothing has changed.

For those waterways that will be removed as a WOTUS, the Tenth Amendment (the states' rights) clearly allows every state to pass their own state legislation to afford the same protections as the EPA did before the redefinition of WOTUS. In other words, all states can do like Arizona was doing when I departed the EPA. They were pursuing state legislation to protect the waterways that were removed with the redefinition with legislation that would protect the waters of Arizona by state law. And in many states, like California, the redefinition essentially didn't change anything, as California has very strong state legislation, like the Porter-Cologne Act, that protects California's waterways, whether it is included as a WOTUS or not.[10]

---

[10] As expected, on July 30, 2021, Biden's EPA and Army Corp of Engineers announced plans to revise the definition of WOTUS (the definition established by the WOTUS rule adopted by the Trump administration) following a process they stated would include two rule makings. A forthcoming foundational rule would restore the regulations defining WOTUS that were in place for decades until 2015, with updates to be consistent with relevant Supreme Court decisions. A separate second rule making process would refine this regulatory

Back to the Office of Wetlands, Oceans, and Watersheds. I provided the background for WOTUS above so the reader will understand why the EPA's traditional focus has not been our oceans. The only relevance our oceans had from a traditional EPA focus was whether there was a connection from inland waterways to the ocean to assert WOTUS's authority pursuant to the Clean Water Act. If there was, you regulated the activity inland.

Whether it was stormwater discharge from a city's streets to the ocean to assert jurisdiction over the city's discharge or an oil company's oil spill into an ephemeral stream to assert jurisdiction over the spill, the EPA's focus was inland—from the source that connected to the ocean—to give jurisdiction for the EPA to regulate pursuant to the Clean Water Act.

So the question is whether the EPA, after fifty years, should now look at our oceans with greater significance from a nonregulatory/enforcement perspective, one that serves the EPA's mission to protect human health and the environment. We now have significant problems with marine debris and microplastics. That debris often washes up on our shores, polluting our beaches. As for microplastics, let me quote an article from *Environmental Sciences Europe* published on April 18, 2018.

> Persistent plastics, with an estimated lifetime for degradation of hundreds of years in marine conditions, can break up into micro- and nanoplastics over shorter timescales, thus facilitating their uptake by marine biota through the food chain. These polymers may contain chemical additives and contaminants, including some known endocrine disruptors that may be harmful at extremely low concentrations for marine biota, thus posing potential risks to marine ecosystems, biodiversity, and food availability.

---

foundation and establish an updated and durable definition of "waters of the United States."

Without immediate strong preventive measures, the environmental impacts and the economic costs are set only to become worse, even in the short term… The quantity observed floating in the open ocean represents only a fraction of the total input: over two-thirds of plastic litter ends up on the seabed with half of the remainder washed up in beaches and the other half floating on or under the surface, so quantifying only floating plastic debris seriously underestimates the amounts of plastics in the oceans.

There are major concentration patches of floating plastics in all the five big ocean gyres, and there is evidence that even the polar areas are acting as additional global sinks of floating plastics.

I am not a scientist, but to make it simple, our plastic, trash, and toxics making its way to our oceans are being consumed by the fish we eat. Toxics and trash on the land lead to everything from Superfund sites at worst to remediation programs at best. Likewise, marine debris and microplastics are leading to a similar situation in our oceans and seabeds. Accordingly, I say the time has come for the EPA to play a much greater role in advocating for clean and healthy ocean initiatives. The natural federal partner is NOAA, the National Oceanic and Atmospheric Administration.

Yes, NOAA is the agency that should take the lead in the federal government's role pertaining to global ocean policy. The EPA, however, whose mission is to protect human health and the environment, should be taking a much greater, more visible role on this issue. Just as EPA worked with its federal partner the Army Corps of Engineers to deal with the WOTUS issue, EPA should be much more active in working with NOAA on the issue of marine debris.

To those who have been strong advocates that the US should be leaders in the global community when it comes to climate change, I ask, where is the passion for a global response to the issue of marine debris and microplastics in our oceans? Our oceans and the fish we consume are being contaminated with toxins and poisons from the marine debris and microplastics that many countries willingly dispose of in the ocean. Asian countries, especially China, are huge culprits. However, every country that has a tributary ending in an ocean is a culprit and needs to be at the table to be part of the solution.

The time has come for the US to take the lead on this issue with more than lip service. The EPA was created and the Clean Water Act was passed to clean up places like the Great Lakes, which was an environmental disaster by the late 1960s. Countries throughout the world are treating our oceans like we once treated our Great Lakes.

There is no scientific debate regarding marine debris being dumped in our oceans, and there is no real debate as to what the outcome is from the toxic and poisons that are dumped into the ocean from that marine debris. So I would urge the new administration to make our oceans and the removal of marine debris and microplastics as much of a global priority as they will climate change. Hopefully, this is something President Biden will prioritize and highlight in future comments he will make to the G7 and G12.

The division for EPA that should be prioritized to deal with this issue is the Office of Wetlands, Oceans, and Watersheds. Those eight or so folks currently assigned to that division fully understand the magnitude of this problem and the need to address the issue as well. Give them the resources they need and deserve. Finally, I want to conclude this chapter with a brief discussion of this division and the role they play related to the federal Coral Reef Task Force.

President Clinton created the Coral Reef Task Force via executive order in 1998. The task force includes representatives from twelve federal agencies; seven US states, territories, and commonwealths; and three freely associated states. The fask force helps build partnerships, strategies, and support for the on-the-ground action to conserve, protect, and enhance coral reefs.

It is cochaired by the assistant secretary of the Office of Insular Affairs and the undersecretary of Commerce for Oceans and Atmosphere, who also serves as the administrator of NOAA. I was the representative on the task force for the US EPA. During my tenure, the cochairs were the deputy secretary of interior, Doug Domenech, and the director of NOAA, Rear Admiral Timothy Gallaudet.

The importance of the task force is seriously overlooked. The task force has established thirteen goals with two themes. The first theme is "Understand Coral Reef Ecosystems." The second theme is "Reduce the Adverse Impacts of Human Activities." When considering these two themes, the reader should understand a plain fact: coral reefs throughout the world are bleaching and dying out. While science may come to different conclusions as to why this is happening, science is not in disagreement that it is happening. The task force is the primary federal vehicle to bring attention to this fact and to support nonprofits, universities, nongovernment organizations (NGOs), and others who are studying the issue and the solutions.

For instance, in Hawaii, at the Hawaii Institute of Marine Biology located on Coconut Island in Kāne'ohe Bay, marine biologists and scientists are studying the super coral reef. These are coral reefs that, for whatever reason, are thriving in ocean waters that have warmed over the last couple of decades. That is significant, as most of the coral reefs that are dying out, such as the Great Barrier Reef off Australia, are in ocean waters where the average water temperature has warmed over the last couple of decades.

This fact has led some to conclude that climate change is causing warmer ocean temperatures, which is resulting in coral reefs dying off. If this hypothesis is correct, the work in Hawaii is critical. They have been studying whether the insertion of DNA from the super coral reef that thrives in warmer waters into the coral reefs that are dying in the warming waters can revive the dying coral reefs. Hopefully, their research will give us some answers.

As for the task force, it really needs to be much more active and engaged with their nonfederal partners to identify solutions to protecting, preserving, and restoring the coral reefs in the oceans of our world. Coral reefs are not just something of beauty for the snorkeler or diver. They buffer shorelines from the effects of hurricanes. They provide protection against flooding and erosion of coastlines. An estimated five hundred million people earn their livelihoods from the fishing stocks and tourism opportunities reefs provide, and the tiny animals that give rise to reefs are even offering hope for new drugs to treat cancer and other diseases.

I felt honored to represent the US EPA on the Coral Reef Task Force. I am hopeful the Biden administration will take the task force and its mission much more seriously than previous Republican or Democrat administrations have, and I hope Biden's EPA will give the task force much greater attention as well. The administrator, the deputy administrator, the assistant administrator for the Office of Water, or the assistant administrator for the Office of International and Tribal Affairs should be representatives on the task force, not a regional administrator.

I served and felt honored to serve because I am an ocean guy. I am a diver and ocean swimmer. I love our oceans. I love our coral reefs. So to be the representative for the US EPA on the task force was personally very meaningful. But the US EPA should be taking the task force much more seriously, and that will start with one of the persons mentioned above serving on the Coral Reef Task Force.

The task force is staffed by the handful of individuals I previously mentioned who work in the Office of Wetlands, Oceans, and Watersheds. They are special people who do so much with so little. In particular, I was extremely impressed by the work of Terri Johnson, who recently retired from the EPA, and Grace Robiou, who is still working for the good of the cause. I hope the new administrator will provide Grace and her colleagues in the OWOW more staff and more resources. Now is the time for EPA to finally step up to the plate and elevate oceans from a policy perspective within EPA.

June 8 of every year is World Oceans Day. I am hopeful the new administrator will make a major announcement in a future World Oceans Day, in conjunction with NOAA, of the role that the US EPA and NOAA will play in addressing negative environmental impacts pertaining to our oceans.

CHAPTER 12

The Real State of the Environment and the Response of the Trump EPA

IN THIS CHAPTER, I would like to address two myths. The first is the myth that the state of the environment continues to worsen. The second myth is that the Trump administration was soft on protecting the environment. I would bet that if you had a focus group of millennials and asked them if the environment was getting safer and cleaner or unhealthier and dirtier, the vast majority would pick the latter option. The fact is, for at least the US, the creation of the EPA by executive order by President Nixon on December 2, 1979, was and is a huge success story.

I grew up in Southern California in the sixties. We lived two miles from the San Gabriel Mountains. During the summer, most of the time, you could not see those mountains because of air pollution. Today, you can see those mountains almost all the time from twenty to thirty miles away.

Here are the facts regarding the state of our environment. In 1970, 40 percent of our nation's drinking water systems failed to meet the most basic clean water standards. Today, over 92 percent of our water systems meet all clean water standards. Between 2003 and 2017, the percentage of people in the US Pacific Island territories receiving safe drinking water increased from 39 percent to 82 percent.

Contrast these to the fact that according to the United Nations, 2.5 billion people around the world lack access to safe drinking water, leading to 1–3 million deaths every year with nearly a thousand children dying every day due to preventable water- and sanitation-related diseases.

With regard to our nation's air quality, from 1970 through 2019, air pollution was reduced by 74 percent while the economy grew by over 285 percent. Between 1990 and 2018, average concentrations of harmful air pollutants decreased considerably across our nation: ground level ozone fell to 21 percent, sulfur dioxide (SO_2) fell to 89 percent, nitrogen dioxide fell to 57 percent, and carbon monoxide fell to 74 percent.

Between 2000 and 2018, fine particulate matter fell to 39 percent. Between 2010 and 2018, lead emissions fell to 82 percent. As for greenhouse gas emissions (GGEs), emissions dropped to 12 percent since 2005. And based on the most recent monitoring data, more than 80 percent of low-income counties were in attainment with EPA's National Ambient Air Quality Standards (NAAQS) compared to 43 percent in 2008. Contrast these facts with the fact that China has seen an increase in air pollution by 50 percent since 2005. More on this fact when I discuss climate change.

As for toxins, since 2007, releases of Toxic Release Inventory (TRI) chemicals, of which more than 650 are reported, have been reduced by 11 percent in air and 20 percent in water. By any standard, the state of the environment in the US is substantially cleaner and healthier than it was before the EPA was created in 1970. For those who insist on the narrative that the sky is falling and that things have gotten so much worse, you simply don't know what you're talking about. The fact is, the creation of the EPA is a success story.

As Americans, we should be proud of the incredible accomplishments we've made in realizing cleaner water, cleaner air, and cleaner land. We should all take a victory lap for how well the EPA ended up serving its mission to protect human health and the environment in its first fifty years. So much for myth number one.

As for that second myth, that the Trump administration was soft on the environment, again, the facts show just the opposite. One natural place to start with to see whether an administration is softer or tougher in regard to the environment is to review whether enforcement actions by the EPA increased or decreased. In Trump's EPA, there was a 48 percent increase in criminal cases for violating environmental laws between 2017 and 2019.

Something I made a top personal priority in Region 9 was focusing on halting the sale of devices designed to defeat required vehicle emissions controls. Essentially, these devices make the catalytic converter useless. The car picks up speed at the expense of becoming a substantial air polluter. For whatever reason, past administrations, including Obama's EPA, chose to do very little in going after the manufacturers or sellers of these devices.

President Trump's EPA stopped the sale of over one million after-market defeat devices. We went from essentially no major defeat device enforcement actions during the Obama administration to making enforcement thanks to a major enforcement action in Region 9, action against the defeat device manufacturer Derive, an EPA national priority in 2018. In Region 9 alone, as I recall, there were five or six major enforcement actions against defeat device manufacturers or distributors in 2019 while I was the RA, and there were ten to eleven in 2020.

On the regulatory front, Trump's EPA was proactive in taking on issues that, again, past administrations chose to punt. As discussed previously in the chapter "The Tribes and the Pacific Island Territories," PFAS had been ignored by every prior administration. The EPA has known about PFAS and has known it is in our drinking water supplies since at least 1995.

To regulate the chemicals in our community's drinking water systems, you have to establish a maximum contaminant level (MCL). Over 550 chemicals have had MCLs established by the EPA. With the MCL established, EPA monitors our drinking water systems to assure the MCL is not exceeded. When it is exceeded, EPA then takes actions to bring the drinking water system into compliance.

In 2018, Trump's EPA acknowledged the problem regarding PFAS and started the process to establish an MCL for PFAS. In 2020, Trump's EPA added PFAS to the Toxic Release Inventory (TRI) previously mentioned. As a result of Trump's EPA, PFAS will finally be monitored in our drinking water systems, and future EPAs will finally be there to assure drinking water does not exceed the PFAS MCL.

As for lead and copper, Trump's EPA finalized the Lead and Copper Rule, which significantly lowered the acceptable levels of lead and copper in our drinking water. This was the first time the EPA reviewed lead and copper levels since 2000. This review was part of Trump's EPA announcing an agency goal of eliminating all lead in our drinking water by the year 2028.

To help accomplish this goal, President Trump's EPA created the first ever Healthy Schools Grant Program, which provides direct funding to our schools to eliminate lead in their drinking water supply. In 2019, $50 million were allocated to our nation's public schools with lead in their drinking water. This is a program that I hope the new administration maintains and that they will even increase the money that can be allocated to our schools.

On the clean air front, it was Trump's EPA to be the first administration to address mobile air sources. Trump's EPA announced the cleaner truck initiative. The cleaner truck initiative will update NOx emissions standards for heavy-duty trucks. It will essentially create uniform maximum emission standards for these trucks in the same way the current standards provide for our cars. Assuming the new administration does not stop the rulemaking process, these standards are expected to be adopted in 2021. If adopted, the standards are expected to reduce truck emissions by 33 percent by 2025.

These new standards will significantly decrease air pollution. This will be especially beneficial in Region 9. The South Coast Air Quality Management District (SCAQMD) and the San Joaquin Valley Air Pollution Control District (SJVAPCD) are two of the largest air districts in the country, and both districts are in nonattainment. Nonattainment means the district is considered to have air quality worse than the National Ambient Air Quality Standards (NAAQS) as defined in Clean Air Act amendments of 1970.

These districts have done a remarkable job in addressing the stationary sources of air pollution within their districts. However, they have no jurisdiction over the mobile sources that pollute within their districts, and these sources are huge polluters. When you think of mobile sources, think of our cars, trucks, trains, planes, and marine vessels.

EPA took on cars years ago and established minimum air emission standards. As a result, new cars are very clean and generate a very small amount of air pollution in our nation's cities, including the SJVAPCD and the SCAQMD. Unfortunately, all past EPA administrations failed to consider adopting air emission standards for trucks, trains, planes, and marine vessels.

With the cleaner truck initiative, Trump's EPA became the first administration in more than forty years to take on one of these other mobile sources. And as I previously mentioned, it will be huge in reducing truck emissions by over 33 percent. I urge Biden's EPA to consider doing the same thing with trains and marine vessels.

The fact is, you have large air districts, like the SCAQMD and SJVAPCD, that cannot accomplish attainment no matter what they do further with their stationary sources. That means the air pollution they get penalized is from the air pollution being generated by sources the federal government can control. In those districts, well over 50 percent of the emissions that put them in nonattainment are from nonstationary sources.

Keep in mind that when a district is in nonattainment, that opens the door for the EPA to step in and direct the district to take actions that can often be very costly. The costs of those actions are then passed on to the residents and businesses in that district. So the end result is, the residents and businesses of a nonattainment district are often strongly penalized for dirty air they have no control over.

Consequently, if the EPA is going to penalize a district for being in nonattainment, it should then step in and regulate all mobile sources that air districts cannot regulate. Trains are huge polluters. As for marine vessels and the SCAQMD, keeping in mind that the Ports of Los Angeles and Long Beach are located within the SCAQMD and that 40 percent of our nation's imports come into these ports from marine vessels, it is estimated that over 40 percent of the emissions that will cause the SCAQMD to be in nonattainment in 2028 will be from marine vessels alone.

Trump's EPA was the first administration in many decades to address mobile sources of air pollution. Hopefully, the new administration will follow up on our administration's efforts in regulating trucks with the establishment of emission standards for trains and marine vessels as well. Only then will several of the air districts in this country be able to achieve attainment.

Personally, I can attest that the only thing ever said to me by anyone in the White House was that the president wanted our EPA to leave a legacy of cleaner air, cleaner water, and a healthier environment. The only thing he wanted was elimination of rules and regulations that did nothing to protect human health or the environment but cost our small businesses money and time, and he wanted more streamlining in the permit application processes.

On the first front, at the time of my departure, Trump's EPA had taken thirty-seven deregulatory actions that will save our nation's small businesses time and over $3 billion annually. On the second front regarding streamlining again, Trump's EPA can be proud of its accomplishments. Concerning water pollution, the backlog of National Pollutant Discharge Elimination System (NPDES) permits, which regulates point sources of pollution in US water, has been reduced by 32 percent since 2017, and Trump's EPA completely eliminated the backlog of EPA actions on the states' list of impaired waters, marking the first time in a decade that this backlog has been eliminated.

Since January 2017, Trump's EPA approved more than seven thousand total maximum daily load (TMDLs) plans to restore polluted waters, a 25 percent increase from the preceding three and a half years. Furthermore, the backlog of actions on state priority TMDLs has fallen dramatically from over one hundred in 2017 to just a single state priority TMDL as of September 2020.

As far as a review of chemicals go, in January 2017, the back-log of new chemicals under review for greater than ninety days had grown to over five hundred. As of September 2020, the number of chemicals under review for greater than ninety days have dropped to less than two hundred, a 60 percent decrease. And since the beginning of President Trump's term in office, EPA had completed over 2,900 new chemical submissions as of September 2020.

So all in all, EPA delivered by the end of President Trump's term in office exactly what the president wanted. Rules and regulations that did nothing to protect human health or the environment were eliminated, saving small businesses money. The permitting process was streamlined, and we have cleaner air, cleaner water, and a healthier environment than when President Trump was first sworn in.

CHAPTER 13

Policy Recommendations for EPA Going Forward

BASED ON MY EXPERIENCES as an EPA regional administrator, I would urge the new administration to give serious consideration to the following policy recommendations. All these recommendations are nonpartisan, and all these recommendations would better serve the mission of the EPA to protect human health and the environment.

Recommendation no. 1. Prioritize delisting or partial delisting Superfund NPL sites in major cities. Once delisted or partially delisted, almost all Superfund NPL sites in major cities will be a prime candidate for brownfield programs. Seek increased annual funding from Congress for the brownfield program. Congress and the EPA prioritizing brownfield projects in major cities means that you will also be serving congressional and EPA environmental justice goals. These sites will almost always be located in an area with an environmental justice focus.

Recommendation no. 2. Reallocate full-time equivalents (FTEs) to regions where EPA's own internal FTE resource allocation assessments acknowledge manpower shortages. For instance, as previously discussed in the chapter "Superfund and Emergency Management," EPA's own internal assessment acknowledged that Region 9 was sixty-one FTEs short based on workload. I advocated aggressively with

HQ for FTEs to be reallocated to Region 9. Unfortunately, it took an inspector general's report acknowledging the same shortfall to get HQ to skeptically start a reallocation.

In November 2019, Peter Wright, the assistant administrator for the Office of Land and Emergency Management (OLEM), agreed to add, as I recall, five additional FTEs in 2020 for Region 9. That is clearly far short of the sixty-one FTEs the EPA's internal assessment concluded should be allocated to Region 9. Unfortunately, the same thing is happening in the Region 9 Office of Air and Radiation.

As discussed in the chapter "The EPA versus California," EPA's own internal FTE allocation assessment concluded that Region 9's Office of Air and Radiation was eighty-one FTEs short. They were short because Region 9 processed more air district state implementation plans (SIPs) than any other region. R9 processes over one hundred a year. Most other regions process under twenty. It is this shortfall of manpower that has caused most of the backlog in SIPs being processed.

It was this same shortfall that caused the problem that Administrator Wheeler attempted to put the blame on California in his letter to California Air Resources Board chair, Mary Nichols. I won't rehash that issue here, but suffice it to say that Region 9's Office of Air and Radiation has a significant shortfall of FTEs.

Hopefully, it won't take an inspector general's report of EPA's FTE allocations in the Office of Air and Radiation to get HQ at EPA to finally respond. I can tell you that anyone from within the EPA who looked at this problem objectively generally agreed that the FTE count within the offices in HQ was high in comparison with the FTE needs throughout the regions.

Recommendation no. 3. As discussed in the chapter "Superfund and Emergency Management," Navajo Nation should become EPA's next substantial geographical program. Geographical programs enable EPA to address health and environmental concerns in a specific area of the country across a set of environmental, economic, cultural, and other conditions common in that area.

Currently, there are four geographical offices. Those offices are for the Chesapeake Bay, the Great Lakes, and the Gulf of Mexico and one for the Office of Mountains, Deserts, and Plains. The first three have a well-defined and well-known area with a full understanding of their environmental challenges and needs. Mountains, deserts, and plains are more generic and doe not meet the traditional criteria of being a "specific area of the country across a set of environmental, economic, cultural, and other conditions common in that area." Navajo Nation would meet those criteria.

As I previously mentioned, I spent a week in Navajo Nation and put 1,200 miles on my car driving from Window Rock to Flagstaff. It is a land of incredible beauty. I don't think anyone who understands the focus of EPA's geographical program and who spent a week in Navajo Nation, as I did, would come to a conclusion other than that Navajo Nation should join the Chesapeake Bay, the Great Lakes, and the Gulf of Mexico as the EPA's next substantial geographical program with its own office.

Recommendation no. 4. Other than the administrator, the person most responsible for assuring that the nation's tribes are given the respect and attention they deserve from the EPA is the assistant administrator of the Office of International and Tribal Affairs (OITA). I have already given you my opinion that the federal agencies do not give our nation's tribes the attention and respect they deserve. This has gone on administration after administration. To assure the EPA does give the respect and attention deserved by our nation's tribes, I strongly recommend that the person nominated by the president to serve as the AA of OITA be a Native American.

Recommendation no. 5. I previously discussed the funding guidance of the General Assistance Program (GAP). To the tribes, this is a huge issue. They spend a great deal of time and resources to apply for GAP funds pursuant to the existing guidance. This guidance was a response to an inspector general report (IGR) that found GAP funds being misallocated.

To respond to the IGR, EPA implemented the current GAP guidance, which places the administrative burden on the tribes that apply for GAP funds and requires the tribes to follow cumbersome and timely requirements to assure that funds are not misallocated. This means less funds are actually allocated to solve environmental problems, as the tribes have to allocate a significant amount of time in the administration and oversight of the GAP funding request.

To respond to the tribe's concerns, I advocated that the GAP guidance be changed to place the burden on the regional office of the EPA to monitor the GAP funds and assure that funds are not misallocated. All my R9 career staff involved with administering GAP fully supported what I proposed. These proposed changes were made available to the tribes for their comments. Most of the tribes strongly supported the changes, as it would require less paperwork and oversight on their part, less manpower to manage the funds, and assure that a greater amount of the funds allocated are spent to better protect the environment.

With Trump's EPA, the review and comment for GAP guidance was carried out by the Office of International and Tribal Affairs (OITA). The OITA spent a great deal of time with public comment and review regarding the potential changes with GAP funding guidance. Unfortunately, in the end, OITA was not able to make a decision, and this issue has been passed on to the new administration. I strongly urge Biden's EPA to adopt the proposed changes to GAP funding guidance. The tribes fully support these changes, and these changes will clearly help the EPA better serve their mission to protect human health and the environment.

Recommendation no. 6. Ninety-two percent of the drinking water in the US is considered safe by all applicable standards. Unfortunately, in the tribal lands, that number is only 73 percent. As the R9 RA, I made it a goal that the percentage of drinking water in R9 tribal lands would be equal to the national average by 2025. I strongly encourage Biden's EPA to adopt this goal as a national goal, that the percentage of drinking water in all tribal lands that is considered safe would be equal to the national percentage.

Recommendation no. 7. Promote and prioritize clean and healthy oceans initiatives. I have mentioned the lack of focus with EPA when it comes to our oceans. I have also discussed the importance of protecting and restoring coral reefs and eliminating marine debris and microplastics. The EPA's Office of Wetlands, Oceans, and Watersheds (OWOW) should be expanded to take on these issues more seriously.

I had been planning to host the first ever Region 9 Clean and Healthy Oceans Summit. We were inviting those who do the research, those who take the action in the field, and those organizations that support their efforts. Our invitees list was a Who's Who from around the world of people, governmental and nongovernmental organizations, and nonprofits that are involved in clean and healthy ocean initiatives. Neither HQ nor any region has ever hosted such a summit.

In January 2020, I was advised that Administrator Wheeler had pulled the plug on my summit. I strongly recommend that Biden's EPA host such a summit. Most of the work has been done. Just reach out to Region 9's Hudson Slay, duty stationed in the Honolulu EPA field office. He did all the work to make sure the summit would be a great success.

Recommendation no. 8. I mentioned in a previous chapter my belief that federal agencies generally do not give our tribes and the Pacific Island territories the attention, respect, or resources they deserve. In that chapter, I give my opinion as to the reason that occurs. With that in mind, I strongly recommend that Administrator Michael Regan visit Navajo Nation and the Pacific Island territories.

Navajo Nation deserves a personal visit from the administrator. Ideally, the administrator could make the visit with a media availability announcing Navajo Nation as EPA's next substantial geographical program with a geographical office!

Likewise, the administrator should personally visit the Pacific Island territories. From my research and from everyone I've spoken with in the territories, no administrator from EPA has ever visited the Pacific Island territories. The administrator from Biden's EPA should be the first administrator to make that visit. The administrator could accompany the president in G7 and G12 summits to the Far East. These summits take place in the Far East usually every other year. The administrator could schedule the trip to the Pacific Island territories on the way to or back from those summits.

Recommendation no. 9. The EPA should place much more emphasis on encouraging and promoting carbon sequestration and carbon capture. This issue of climate change evolves around greenhouse gas emissions. Carbon is a huge component in those emissions. I have seen friendships destroyed over this issue, so here is my take.

Climate change exists. It was initially called global warming, but the advocates chose to change that name, as it was clear that many places in the world were cooling. In any event, the argument is that science has proven that greenhouse gas emissions and carbon created by man have caused what was initially called global warming but now is called climate change.

I am not a scientist, but I acknowledge that climate change exists. There are those who say that science is empirical and prove that climate change is 100 percent anthropogenic. On that front, I disagree. Climate change does exist. I do not, however, believe that science can accurately attribute a percentage of fault to either human activity or natural events, such as forest fires and volcanic eruptions.

But here is what I do know and what I hope could rally all the believers and nonbelievers when it comes to climate change. What I do know for a fact is that the amount of carbon dioxide in our atmosphere is not healthy. The mission of the EPA is to protect human health and the environment. To better protect human health, we should all be supportive of policies that reduce carbon emissions in the air not for the political cause of climate change but for a cause I think we would all support: a healthier environment.

It is for this reason that I believe everyone involved in this debate would support international agreements with other countries that would commit the US to reducing our greenhouse gas and carbon emissions so long as China, India, and the other developed countries have the exact same requirements imposed on their air emissions. As stated earlier, while the air pollution in the US has been reduced by 73 percent since 1973, China's air pollution has doubled since 2000. If you truly believe that man is causing climate change, then you should fully support a framework that requires all the developed countries, including China and India, to commit to what every other developed country has done in the Kyoto treaty.

Unfortunately, pursuant to the Kyoto treaty, China was treated like an undeveloped country and was allowed to increase their air emissions until the year 2025, which would be considered the baseline year, and their emission reductions would start from that point forward. In other words, they were encouraged to be a gross air polluter and to have the highest emissions possible in 2025, which would be used as their baseline.

As stated previously, the US is not the problem. All our numbers have gone down. We wouldn't be having this debate if all the other countries of the world had the same emission reductions as the US. So I say to all those so active in the cause, let's unite in having an international treaty that requires all developed countries, including China and India, to have the same emission reductions in an agreement that is considered enforceable.

We should all support this course of action for a simple reason. Carbon emissions are unhealthy. Whether or not this treaty will do something to affect climate change, only time will tell. But I can assure you, there will be a much healthier environment in terms of air pollution and a significant reduction in asthma and other pulmonary diseases.

So back to carbon sequestration and capture. I find it odd that the people and organizations so involved with the climate change issue and that want to shut down the carbon-oriented energy market have done absolutely nothing to promote policies encouraging carbon sequestration or capture. You hear the term climate change all the time. You watch on the news President Biden appointing a climate change czar, John Kerry. You see the president, by executive order, kill the Keystone Pipeline. It is, "Stop this project," and, "Stop that project."

Have you, however, ever heard the president mention the words carbon sequestration and carbon capture? Pretty sure that is a big no, and that's sad because those two phrases mean absorbing into the soils or capturing through various processed tons of emissions of carbon. If you really believe that carbon and man have caused climate change and you want to change it, you should be all in, in supporting comprehensive programs to support carbon capture and carbon sequestration.

A ton of carbon that you remove from the atmosphere through shutting down a factory is no greater than a ton of carbon you absorb into the soils through sequestration or through a mechanical process through capture. For the proponents of this movement to not be actively supporting sequestration and capture as much as factory closure is pure political BS and hypocrisy.

So for the Biden EPA, which has made it very clear that climate change will be a huge priority, I strongly recommend that the Biden administration elevate the issue of carbon capture and carbon sequestration. I tried to elevate the issue of sequestration and got nowhere. What I can tell you is, the US EPA has very few, if any, resources and little staff allocated for this issue. If climate change is going to be a big issue for President Biden, then that means it will be a big issue for Biden's EPA. If that is the case, then they should not neglect the benefits that can be derived in addressing this issue via carbon capture and carbon sequestration. Carbon sequestration and carbon capture should become a top priority for Biden's EPA. That will help serve the mission of the EPA, whether it is to protect human health, the environment, or both.

Recommendation no. 10. As stated previously, thanks to President Trump, Speaker Pelosi and the stakeholders along the US-Mexico border at the San Diego-Tijuana sector now have appropriations of $350 million to spend on the US side of the border to deal with transboundary sewage. However, the rest of the border has pretty much been ignored.

I tried to make addressing this issue from the Rio Grande and the Gulf of Mexico in Texas to the Pacific Ocean in San Diego, California, an EPA national priority. I failed. What could have been a huge environmental win for Trump's EPA became something that, fortunately, others can take credit for. I would be remiss if I did not personally extend my huge gratitude to Speaker Pelosi. Without her support, this would not have happened.

In any event, now is the time for Biden's EPA to do what Trump's EPA should have. Now is the time to address the issue along the entire border. From the initial assessments Region 9 (California and Arizona) and Region 6 (Texas and New Mexico) did, the cost to address this issue outside the San Diego-Tijuana sector would be significantly less than the $350 million appropriated just for that sector.

This is a huge issue. It is an environmental disaster. The people living in border communities, such as Nogales and Naco, are not having their health and environment protected from transboundary sewage. We talk about securing the border. Well, if politics precludes an agreement on that issue, let's try to get an agreement on environmentally securing the border. That should be something Republicans, Democrats, and Independents can all rally behind. It is time for people living on the US side of the US-Mexico border to not wake up tomorrow morning worrying about being subjected to sewage from Mexico being in their backyards and streams.

Recommendation no. 11. Give Navajo Nation a greater voice in the processes that will be used in remediating the Superfund NPL abandoned uranium mines (AUM), and give Navajo Nation a greater voice in awarding the contracts that will be awarded over the next thirty years with regard to the Superfund NPL AUM remediation work.

Superfund remediation work normally involves very complicated and highly technical mechanical processes. The engineering work that goes into these processes is mind-boggling. The remediation work of AUMs will no doubt, in many cases, utilize these traditional processes. However, the EPA needs to keep an open mind in considering natural processes for remediation that the Navajo Nation Superfund division may advocate for.

As previously discussed, the Navajo native people, in line with hózhó, advocate for peace, balance, beauty, and harmony with Mother Earth. It is critically important that the EPA go forward with the remediation of the AUMs with an acknowledgment of how important hózhó is to the Navajo Nation people. It is important because consistent with the belief of hózhó, natural processes are less offensive to Mother Earth than large, complicated, and highly technical processes that will be built in or on the mountains where the AUMs are located.

If it takes these traditional, mechanical processes to remediate, then fine. But if a natural process can potentially remediate as well and Navajo Nation Superfund advocates for that process, it is critical that EPA have a serious dialogue with Navajo Nation Superfund regarding that alternative.

As for the contractors who will do the work, it is vitally critical that Navajo Nation have an equal seat with EPA at the table when it comes to awarding contracts. There is $1.8 billion in the Tronox trust fund, which will be used to dole out hundreds of millions of dollars in contracts over the next thirty years. The first contract was recently awarded for $220 million. Representatives of Navajo Nation did not feel like the EPA worked very closely with them in the award of that contract. The Biden EPA must assure that Navajo Nation is a full and equal partner going forward during the bidding process and in the award of the contracts.

The Biden EPA needs to sit down with Navajo Nation to discuss ways that prime contractors who list Navajo Nation subcontractors in their bid will be more favorably rated for purposes of the award. The fact is, these projects are so complicated that currently, there are no Navajo Nation companies that would be eligible to bid as a prime contractor. Hopefully, over the next decade, that will change.

To assure that the greatest number of Navajo Nation companies get AUM work, the best way is to score prime contractor bids higher if they have those companies listed in their bid. In other words, if two prime contractors come in with relatively the same bid, the company that has the greater number of Navajo Nation companies listed as subcontractors gets awarded the bid.

The Navajo Nation will be contending with remediation of the AUMs for decades to come. This situation is because our country obtained all the uranium used for our nation's defense from the AUMs in the Navajo Nation, and the people of Navajo Nation are now paying the price. Fundamental basics of environmental justice require the EPA to work with Navajo Nation as an equal partner going forward in the processes that will be used to remediate and the contractors who will be awarded the AUM work.

Recommendation no. 12. Biden's EPA should adopt five- and ten-year business plans regarding the attraction and retention of future employees. There is a big difference between the employees hired in the seventies, eighties, and nineties and those being hired today. The people hired decades ago had more of a commitment to being EPA lifers. They accepted the job with a commitment, wanting to serve the mission of the EPA until they retired. Today, it is not uncommon for well over half of those being hired to look for higher-paying jobs five years later. And I can assure you that 90 percent of the people who get hired by the EPA can find a much larger paycheck five years later in the private sector.

And then there is the issue of the cost of living. In Region 9, the HQ is in downtown San Francisco. San Francisco has one of the highest cost of living indexes in the country, and if you look at most other regions, their HQ is also located in a city with a high cost of living.

To better attract prospective employees, the EPA needs to start assessing downsizing the number of employees working at the regional HQ and expanding the number of employees working in field offices in that region. For instance, in Region 9, I was advocating with HQ that they seriously consider over the next five years adding a couple hundred employee spots to the LA field office. LA has a high cost of living, but it's nowhere near as high as San Francisco.

I also suggested that the LA field office be moved to Glendale, which is five miles away from Downtown LA, where costs are even lower. With these additional spots for employees, prospective R9 employees could be recruited with the understanding that they would be hired, spend the first six months in San Francisco, and then be duty stationed to the LA field office.

This approach should be duplicated in each of the other regions to move employees out of the HQ in Region 10 or Region 2, in Seattle or New York respectively, and expand the staffing capacity in their field offices. If the EPA were to do this, they would have a much easier time recruiting and retaining new employees. This is a much bigger issue than you think. The fact is, because those hired decades ago wanted to serve until they retired, an exceptionally high percentage of current EPA employees are eligible for retirement.

I believe that in Region 9, that number is approaching almost 60 percent of the entire workforce. I expect that President Biden's EPA will see a large number of employees retiring over the next couple of years. To fill the void, the EPA needs to come up with a business plan to address this issue. I strongly believe a component of that plan should include downsized HQs in the regions and upsized field offices with a lower cost of living index.

Finally, a component of this business plan should be to reverse Trump's EPA policy of decreasing the amount of time EPA employees can telework from home. We just went through a year of COVID with governmental and nongovernmental businesses clearly establishing that you can get things done by teleworking from home. Trump's EPA was at odds with unions representing EPA's employees over the issue of teleworking. Trump's EPA attempted to decrease the amount of telework time.

Biden's EPA needs to embrace the concept of teleworking. Providing more time to telework from home will help in the attraction and retention of employees, and it will free up space. In Region 9, the federal government is spending taxpayer dollars to lease nineteen of twenty floors of a downtown San Francisco high-rise. With a teleworking policy allowing all employees to telework two to three days a week from home, you could potentially cut that space down from one-third to one-half of the current space.

If you take this approach throughout the federal government with all federal agencies, there would be a reduction of hundreds of millions, if not billions, of dollars in federal costs for leased buildings to do business. In Region 9, it certainly would be a huge savings, which could be money that goes into projects to give us clean air, water, and land. And it could be huge for attracting and retaining the next generations of EPA employees, who will be carrying out the EPA mission to protect human health and the environment.

Recommendation no. 13. Biden's EPA needs to finalize the cleaner truck regulations that Trump's EPA initiated to establish emission standards for trucks, and it should immediately commence rulemaking to additionally promulgate regulations to establish emission standards for trains and marine vessels as well.

With the establishment of emission standards for these three mobile sources, air districts in nonattainment will have real opportunities to move into attainment. Again, keep in mind that these districts are severely punished for being in nonattainment but have absolutely no control over these mobile sources of air pollution. Furthermore, these mobile sources are a substantial contributor to the air emissions that cause these districts to be in nonattainment.

Recommendation no. 14. Stormwater discharge and runoff is a major environmental problem in almost every major US coastal city. In R9, that means Honolulu, Los Angeles, and San Francisco. I discussed in detail the situation involving San Francisco and my issuing a notice of violation (NOV) in October 2019. In August 2010, the city of Honolulu entered into a consent decree with the EPA for the same reasons.

The bottom line is that most of our major cities built sewer systems designed for the fifties. Seventy years later, these cities just won't have the infrastructure to handle the discharge caused by normal rain events. The stormwater overflows in the sewers, the wastewater treatment facilities become overwhelmed in these events, and water flows where gravity takes it, ultimately ending up in the surrounding ocean or bay. In the course of the flow trash, raw sewage, hazardous household wastes, pesticides, etc. flow into people's homes and businesses before making it to the final discharge into the ocean or bay.

These cities all want to address the issue but don't have anywhere near the financial resources to build the infrastructure necessary to address the need. Accordingly, with limited financial resources, our major coastal cities are taking a Band-Aid approach to a huge problem.

Under the Clean Water Act's National Pollutant Discharge Elimination System (NPDES) program, EPA regulates discharges of pollutants from municipal and industrial wastewater treatment plants, sewers, collection systems, and stormwater discharges. The Clean Water Act requires that industrial facilities, construction sites, and municipal separate storm sewer systems (MS4s) have measures in place to prevent pollution from being discharged with the stormwater into the nearby waterways. Unfortunately, as a result of the lack of necessary stormwater and wastewater infrastructure, these discharges take place on a regular basis, subjecting these municipalities to EPA enforcement actions.

To address this situation, Congress needs to appropriate substantial funding. The money should be appropriated to the EPA's Water Infrastructure Finance and Innovation Act (WIFIA) budget. For fiscal year 2021, approximately $5.5 billion was allocated by Congress to the EPA for all eligible WIFIA projects. Congress, going forward, should appropriate a specific amount to the WIFIA budget allocation solely for stormwater discharge projects in our nation's cities.

There is a lot of talk these days in DC to address infrastructure. President Trump unsuccessfully attempted to get an infrastructure bill through Congress. Now President Biden is attempting to accomplish the same thing. Many of these proposals include billions of dollars for things that have nothing, in my opinion, to do with infrastructure.[11]

For members of Congress reading this, I strongly believe any true infrastructure legislation should include appropriations to address the transboundary sewage problem, which was not addressed with the $350 million appropriation previously discussed to respond at the San Diego-Tijuana sector at the US-Mexico border, and appro-

---

[11] Infrastructure Legislation Update. On October 1, 2021, the Senate gave overwhelming bipartisan approval on Tuesday to a $1 trillion infrastructure bill to rebuild the nation's deteriorating roads and bridges and fund new climate resilience and broadband initiatives, delivering a key component of President Biden's agenda. The vote, 69 to 30, was uncommonly bipartisan. The yes votes included Senator Mitch McConnell of Kentucky, the Republican leader, and 18 other Republicans. The measure faces a potentially rocky and time-consuming path in the House, where Speaker Nancy Pelosi and a majority of the nearly 100-member Progressive Caucus have said they will not vote on it unless and until the Senate passes a separate, even more ambitious $3.5 trillion social policy bill. With $550 billion in new federal spending, the measure supported in the Senate would provide $65 billion to expand high-speed internet access; $110 billion for roads, bridges, and other projects; $25 billion for airports; and the most funding for Amtrak since the passenger rail service was founded in 1971. As of the date of publication of this book no infrastructure bill had been passed and signed into law. More significantly, in regard to responding to the transboundary sewage problem at the US-Mexico border, NO funding had been proposed or earmarked for dealing with this problem in any of the infrastructure legislation proposals.

priations to our nation's cities to address stormwater discharge infrastructure needs by allocating the necessary dollars to our major cities.

Recommendation no. 15. The administrator for the US EPA should restore the position of special adviser to the administrator for the states and regions. This was a position created by Administrator Pruitt, and it improved the ability of the EPA to serve the mission of protecting human health and the environment. This position, while filled by Ken Wagner, significantly improved communications between the US EPA and the states. More importantly, it filled a void between the regions with the regional administrator and headquarters and the politically appointed staff.

It is easy in the federal bureaucracy for those in Washington, DC, to forget about the real world out in the regions. This position helped bridge that gap. Administrator Wheeler eliminated the position. Administrator Regan should restore it.

Recommendation no. 16. Some will look at my final recommendation as humorous, but I actually think it is very important. Biden's EPA should create the Alexis Strauss Excellence in EPA award. Alexis Strauss worked for every Region 9 regional administrator who served in that capacity since the creation of the EPA in 1970. She retired in September 2019. She is one of the most knowledgeable persons on what the EPA is all about. Whatever success I can claim as a regional administrator, I owe much of it to Ms. Strauss. When she retired, the EPA truly lost the best of the best.

The EPA has national awards named after former EPA career staff. They are named after those individuals because of the incredible work those individuals performed on a daily basis in carrying out the mission of the EPA. The next award to be named after a former employee should be named after Alexis Strauss.

If the administrator of Biden's EPA does not want to pursue this course of action, then the next R9 regional administrator should make this a regional award. I had made plans with my deputy regional administrator, Deborah Jordan, and assistant regional administrator, Kerry Drake, to award the first Alexis Strauss Excellence in EPA to Ms. Strauss at the fiftieth anniversary event that we were planning for December 2020. In the aftermath of my firing and with the onset of

COVID-19, that event did not take place, and the award was never created.

It's time to create the award today. After Ms. Strauss, I was going to create an award to allow the Region 9 senior division staff to annually decide whether there was any former career or political EPA staff who was deserving of the award. It was not an annual award but an award that would have been given out any year to whomever the senior division staff agreed should be so recognized.

CHAPTER 14

My Termination, the Litigation, and Going Forward

I MAY NEVER KNOW the reason why I was terminated, but I have my suspicions, which I will discuss in this chapter. One thing I do know for a fact is, I wasn't fired for the reasons stated. Two days after the firing, the EPA released a public statement stating the following:

> Mike was too interested in travel for the sake of travel and ignored necessary decision-making required of a regional administrator. Although EPA leadership repeatedly requested Mike to simply conduct the basic responsibilities of his job, we regretfully and ultimately after many requests had to relieve him for severe neglect and incompetent administration of his duties.

That I can assure you is false, defamatory, and an outright lie, as my attorney stated to Andrew Wheeler, Doug Benevento, Ryan Jackson, and Corry Schiermeyer in a letter dated December 17.

> The aforesaid statements were deliberately made knowing they were false and, therefore,

were made with malice. Indeed, the EPA has Travel Guidance Rules that must be adhered to and followed by all EPA employees to assure that what you alleged Mr. Stoker did cannot happen. You are all aware of those rules.

In the case of Mr. Stoker, those rules required that all travel must first be approved by the Deputy Regional Administrator (DRA) or the Assistant Regional Administrator (ARA). In every instance all travel taken by Mr. Stoker was approved by either the DRA or the ARA. As a backup to ensuring those rules are adhered to all travel approved by the DRA or the ARA must then finally be approved by the EPA Travel Office located in Cincinnati.

Again, in regards to Mr. Stoker, every trip he took was approved by the EPA Travel Office assuring all EPA Travel Guidance Rules were followed. Notwithstanding each of you were aware of those rules, knew those rules were being enforced and knew there was no travel Mr. Stoker was involved with that violated those rules, you published the false statements referenced above.

We believe these rules are of such legal significance that we are confident we would prevail as a matter of law in a summary judgment action with the court concluding that no individual could do what you alleged Mr. Stoker did without violating the EPA Travel Guidance Rules. As no rules were violated, as a matter of law, it would be impossible to do what you alleged were the reasons for Mr. Stoker's termination.

Also evidencing the falsity of the public statements concerning Mr. Stoker are Mr. Jackson's pre-2020 statements to the media. Mr. Jackson repeatedly and publicly maintained that Mr. Stoker's travel was a required part of his job, which he was performing satisfactorily. Mr. Jackson responded to several news agencies and stated that Mr. Stoker's frequent travel was expected of him, that had no issues regarding his travel and that his work was "very portable."

Further, several individuals within the EPA defended Mr. Stoker's travel and working remotely. To wit, EPA spokesman Michael Abboud stated, "EPA carefully evaluated Regional Administrator Stoker's schedule, travel, and work for the past year and where a suitable duty station for him should be… Mr. Stoker spends part of his time in EPA offices in California and the rest traveling between the 8 time zones and 148 tribes that encompass Region 9, serving its 50 million residents with 22 million in Southern California alone."

Additionally, a news reporter with a national publication will testify that at approximately 5:00 pm EST on February 6, 2020, he spoke with Mr. Abboud and specifically asked, "[Was] travel any part of the reason for Mr. Stoker's termination?" To which Mr. Abboud responded, "[Absolutely] not." This conversation took place approximately three (3) hours before Ms. Schiermeyer publicly disseminated the defamatory statements.

Finally, we believe the recklessness of your collective actions is also demonstrated by the fact, according to reliable sources, that you did not even consult with the EPA's General Counsel, Matt Leopold. Any attorney would counsel their employer client in a termination matter involving an "at-will" employee to not state any reason for terminating the employee.

> We are confident that the evidence will
> show the Mr. Leopold was not consulted. Had he
> been consulted he would have given the advice to
> state no reason for the termination. And if you
> collectively still insisted on stating a reason, he
> would have requested the background informa-
> tion you were basing your allegation upon. Since
> that background information does not exist Mr.
> Leopold would have correctly advised you to not
> issue the defamatory statements.
>
> The fact the four (4) of you did not even
> seek out advice of your counsel is evident reck-
> lessness and malice each of you had in wanting
> to use false and defamatory statement regarding
> Mr. Stoker. As a result of the statements and
> the reckless nature in which they were public
> disseminated Mr. Stoker need not prove special
> damages as you all engaged in slander "per se"
> by charging a professional person with general
> incompetence.[12]

The letter speaks for itself. The letter was sent in an attempt
to settle the matter. The four individuals were being advised that a
defamation lawsuit seeking punitive damages against each would be
pursued. I had made it clear to reporters immediately following my
firing that I would not be taking any action that could negatively
affect the president. I am old-fashioned, and I believe that when a
governor or a president appoints you to a high position, you don't
write books, say anything negative about the administration, or file
lawsuits until that governor or president is no longer in office.

President Trump left office on January 20, 2021. On January
27, 2021, my attorney filed a complaint against the aforenamed individuals for defamation. In terms of the damages my attorney is seeking, the December 17 letter summarized that to the four individuals.

---

[12] Miles v. Perry (1987) 11 Conn.App.584, 602.

Damages Mr. Stoker is entitled to damages for: (1) Harm to his business, trade, profession, or occupation; (2) Harm to his reputation; and for (3) Shame, mortification, or hurt feelings, among others. (See CACI 1700.)

The ripple effects of having multiple news agencies report that Mr. Stoker was relieved of his duties with the EPA due to "severe neglect and incompetent administration of his duties" are widespread and far reaching.

Mr. Stoker lost his annual salary of $192,000. Despite his best efforts, Mr. Stoker has not been able to secure comparable employment, which is a direct consequence of the American public, potential employers and clients being recklessly misinformed by the EPA that he was incompetent and severely neglectful in his duties as a Regional Administrator.

As a result of these actions it is likely that Mr. Stoker will not be able to find comparable employment for the remainder of his working career. Moreover, and as is the case for most working professionals, Mr. Stoker expected substantial increases in his future annual income by reason of his accumulated experience/knowledge and prestige as the EPA's Region 9 Administrator. Conservatively, our retained economist calculates Mr. Stoker's future lost income at $960,000 over the next seven (7) years. Further, we value the harm to Mr. Stoker's reputation and his shame well into the six figures.

Should we pursue all available remedies at law, we believe that the following damages would be proven at a minimum.

Past Economic Loss $192,000
Future Economic Loss $960,000

Harm to Reputation $200,000
Feeling of Shame $50,000
Punitive Damages $1,500,000
Total $2,902,000

While I do not know if the real reasons for my termination will come out through litigation, I do know that we will clearly prove it was not for the reasons they gave. It is significant that two weeks after issuing the defamatory statement, I emailed the four defendants in late March 2020 and advised them that if they retracted the statement and acknowledged it was false, I would waive all rights to pursue any causes of action against them.

This was never about money. It was about fighting for my good name and reputation. They never responded to the email. Therefore, as promised, I pursued my only course of action to clear my name with the filing of the complaint in federal district court.[13]

---

[13] Litigation Status Update. On January 27, 2021, I filed a defamation lawsuit in the United States District Court for the Central Division of the State of California against former Administrator Wheeler and three other high level political appointees of the President. (Case 2:21-cv-00733) Prior to the filing of my Complaint, Jean Carroll filed a defamation case against the President of the United States in the United States District Court, S.D. New York. (Case 20-cv-7311). In both cases United States of America, has attempted to substitute out the individually named defendants and substitute in the United State of America as the defendant on the assertion that the defendants (Wheeler et. al. in my case and the President in the Carrol case) were acting in the course and scope of authority as employees of the United States of America. The US Attorney's in both cases have relied upon 28 U.S.C. Section 2679 (d) (1) which provides, "... upon certification by the Attorney General that the employee was acting within the scope of his office or employment at the time of the incident..." the United States shall be substituted as the party defendant. On October 26, 2020, U.S. District Court Judge Lewis A. Kaplan ruled that allegations of defamation by Carroll, which must be assumed as fact for purposes of determining what can or cannot be conduct protected as within the course and scope of employment, were NOT protected. Specifically, it was noted that it would be counter to public policy to allow federal employees who intentionally lie or falsify information to not be held accountable for their intentional actions. The US Attorney's Office appealed that decision up to the 2nd Circuit. That matter is set for Oral Argument on December 3, 2021. On June 24, 2021, U.S. District

So why was I terminated? I believe it started when Doug Benevento was appointed to replace Ken Wagner, who had left to become the secretary of Energy and Environment in the state of Oklahoma. Doug's new position included being the liaison between regional administrators to HQ and to the administrator. I reached out with an issue I had brought to Ryan Jackson's attention and also left voice messages, which he never responded to. Emailing Ryan Jackson was not an option, as they were subject to the media getting the copy through a Freedom of Information Act, so we communicated with voice mails.

Doug was now on the job, and I had a real concern involving one of my employees. Jackson ignored it, so now it was time to see what Doug could do. Ultimately, I believe this issue and how Jackson

---

Court Judge John A. Kronstadt, ruled that defamatory statements of Wheeler, et. al. are deemed to be within the course and scope of employment as a result of the United States of America, through the U.S. Attorneys, invoking 28 USC Section 2679 (d) (1). In his ruling all allegations of intentionally lying and stating false facts by the defendants were assumed to be true. On September 7, 2021, I filed my Notice of Appeal with the 9th Circuit. My Opening Brief with the 9th Circuit must be filed by November 12, 2021. Among other arguments, my attorneys are arguing that Congress did not intend for 28 USC 2679 (d) (1) to be applied to protect egregious and intentional wrongful conduct by federal employees, that it is contrary to public policy to protect intentional wrong doing by federal employees by invoking 28 USC 2679 (d) (1) and that to not allow an individual to have his or her day in court and have the matter adjudicated on the merits is a denial of due process. Significantly, the United States of America, pursuant to legislation passed by Congress, is immune from defamation lawsuits. Consequently, once the individually named defendants are successfully substituted out and the United States of America is substituted in as the defendant, the US Attorneys next action would be to file a Motion to Dismiss which would be granted. Therefore, if that is the ultimate outcome in both my case and the Carroll case we would never have be given the opportunity to prove our defamation claims which is the basis for claiming a denial of due process. Clearly, these two cases are on a potential path for one or both cases being consolidated to have this matter ultimately adjudicated by the United States Supreme Court. For members of Congress reading this book, I would strongly urge you to consider authoring legislation that specifically excludes intentional torts from being considered as withing the course and scope of employment for purposes of 28 USC 2679 (d) (1).

and Benevento responded, in hindsight, were the beginning of my end as a regional administrator.

I had an employee whom I previously mentioned, Charles Munoz. Charles had worked on the presidential campaign and professed to have come into close contact with then Mr. Donald Trump. (We were told they named their firstborn after Mr. Trump's wife.) Within weeks after becoming President Trump, the first political appointment for the EPA was Charles Munoz.

President Trump appointed Charles Munoz as the EPA's White House liaison. All federal agencies have a politically appointed White House liaison. For EPA, that would be Charles. After meeting with Administrator Pruitt and his COS, Ryan Jackson, to discuss my becoming the R9 regional administrator, Jackson then took me to Munoz to start processing me in.

Two months later, I arrived in San Francisco to be sworn in on May 18, 2018. Charles was there to meet me. To my surprise, Jackson and HQ had transferred him to R9 and had allowed his duty station to be Las Vegas, where a national EPA field office was located. Significantly, there is no R9 field office in Vegas. There had once been one, but it had been closed long before Munoz was transferred to R9.

From the very outset, this issue became a major concern of mine. I discussed it with Alexis Strauss, Deborah Jordan, and Amy Miller. We all had the same concern, believing an R9 employee needed to be duty stationed in an R9 office. The one thing that gave me comfort was when I was advised that HQ was still paying all travel for Mr. Munoz. Knowing that, I left Jackson another voice message.

I stated that while HQ was okay with a regional employee not being duty stationed in a regional office, I had major concerns. I had been advised that Mr. Munoz was still doing work for HQ from Vegas. Knowing that and the fact that HQ was picking up Munoz's travel expenses, I advised Jackson that I expected him to do Mr. Munoz's end-of-the-year performance review. I wanted to make sure that the record was clear that I considered Munoz primarily as an HQ staffer and not a regional one, and I wanted to make sure I did nothing to expressly or impliedly suggest that I signed off on this arrangement.

Munoz continued to work out of Vegas, and Jackson did his 2018 end-of-the-year performance review, and then I was advised by Deborah Jordan and Alexis Strauss in March 2019 of troubling news. I was advised that HQ had quit paying Mr. Munoz's travel expenses. Essentially, HQ had severed any nexus between them and Munoz, leaving him exclusively now as an R9 employee.

I then confronted Mr. Munoz and told him I had major concerns. I felt that this would have no other ending but a bad one. I told him that I was going to lobby HQ to support my position of wanting him to properly be duty stationed in an R9 office. Mr. Munoz wasn't happy about that but said he understood my concerns. He told me his lease was not up until September 1, 2019. I told him I would be asking HQ to support me in requiring him to have an R9 duty station effective on September 1, 2019.

I then followed up with a voice message to Mr. Jackson stating that I had strong objections to Munoz being in the Vegas office and not in an R9 office. I told him I was requesting his support for requiring Munoz to duty station in an R9 office effective on September 1, 2019. I left another message stating pretty much the same thing in April. I received no response.

Benevento was now on the job, and so I made the call to Doug. I told Doug I needed his help with an HQ issue. I then briefed him on the Munoz situation and the fact that Jackson wasn't responding. He initially fully understood my concern. I reminded him that Munoz had been the first appointed in the EPA by the president. I said it was inconceivable to me that the media wouldn't jump on this story. He told me he would talk to Jackson.

In May or June, I called Benevento again to discuss this issue, and he told me he would follow up. That implied to me that there had not been a conversation with Jackson up to that point. I was back in DC in early July. RAs would often use a side room next to Benevento's as an office while in DC. I was in that side room when Benevento came into his office. We said our hellos. I then brought up the Munoz situation.

Doug, with a firm look, said, "Mike, Ryan Jackson doesn't have a problem with Charles being in Vegas. I don't have a problem with Charles being in Vegas. And we don't want you to have a problem with Charles being in Vegas." That was basically all that was said about Munoz. I was livid, and I advised Deborah Jordan and Alexis Strauss what had happened. They knew I was working on moving Munoz into an R9 office on September 1, 2019.

I advised them about what Benevento had said. We were all disappointed, as we were all very concerned with what could happen as a result of this conversation. We concluded that I needed to document in as many nonemail ways as possible that this was on HQ, Jackson, and Wheeler, who had to approve Munoz's duty station in Vegas. And I needed to document in as many ways as possible that I was opposed to the arrangement.

At that point, my main concern was the media picking this story up and running with a theme that Munoz, because of his close relationship with the president, was being given preferential treatment. Bottom line and common sense should dictate that a regional EPA employee is duty stationed in a regional office. It's a pretty simple concept, but if the media got ahold of bits and pieces of this story, it would not end well for Munoz or me or Wheeler or Trump's EPA. Boy, was I wrong. A bad media story would have been much better than what was about to come.

A couple of weeks later, I was in San Francisco for the week. Munoz, Alexis Strauss, and I went into a meeting with Senator Feinstein's chief of staff in her San Francisco office. After the meeting, we walked back to our R9 office. My COS had added a meeting to my calendar that included Mr. Munoz, myself, and the EPA's inspector general. Let me be clear. It is not uncommon for regional administrators to meet with the IG to discuss issues they are looking into. They are fairly routine. There was nothing to indicate to me, Munoz, or my staff that this would be any different.

I believe the meeting was set for 10:00 a.m. Munoz came to my office, and we walked out to meet what I thought would be one IG. Much to my surprise, down the hall, we were met by four IGs. They approached us, and two grabbed Munoz and took him to a conference room on the other side of the building. Two grabbed me and took me into my conference room, which was located right next to my office. As for IG representation, two were from HQ, and two were from R9, and these four were all from the enforcement division.

They sat me down, and the IG proceeded to read me, for the first time in my life, my Miranda rights. They started by saying that the purpose of the meeting was as a criminal investigation for fraud involving an R9 employee whose name was Charles Munoz. They read me my rights, and I initialed a Miranda rights form and acknowledged that I understood my rights, and then the questioning began.

I believe my interview took somewhere between thirty and forty-five minutes. I advised them that Munoz was in Vegas when I started the job. I underscored that he continued to work for HQ. I also told them that Jackson, not I, had approved his arrangement. I told them I knew nothing about the duty station agreement he had with HQ. (I had no clue and still am in the dark to this day whether there was such an agreement.) I made it clear that if there was any agreement, Jackson would be aware of it. I also underscored that it was Jackson who performed his 2018 end-of-the-year performance review.

We essentially ended the meeting at this point. It was apparent that their main focus, for whatever reason, was 2018. Fortunately, they didn't prod into 2019. So my voice messages to Jackson, my conversations with Benevento, the directive Benevento gave to me to not make it an issue, and my expressing to both of them my concerns and wanting to reassign Munoz's duty station to an R9 office effective on September 1, 2019 never came up.

That was the last I heard from the IG while being the RA. I left a voice message for Jackson and Benevento stating what had happened. On March 31, 2021, the inspector general's office issued a report concluding that Munoz and Ryan engaged in fraudulent payroll activities. They also concluded that Munoz and Jackson submitted official timesheets and personnel forms that contained materially false, fictitious, and fraudulent statements to mislead EPA personnel and facilitate improper payments over multiple months. It also found that Munoz received an improper raise and submitted "fraudulent timesheets" in regard to working out of the Las Vegas EPA office. The IG report concluded that the fraud committed by Munoz cost the EPA almost $96,000. While the justice department has declined to prosecute Jackson or Munoz, Inspector General Sean O'Donnell has said, "The EPA Office of Inspector General will do everything within its power to ensure that public officials are held accountable for acts of misconduct during their service." A spokesperson for EPA Administrator Michael Regan has stated, "The agency is evaluating the report and potential next steps."

In my mind and gut, the Munoz issue was the beginning of my end. I believe that instead of Jackson and Benevento viewing my approach as troubleshooting, being proactive, or bottom line, protecting the president from unwanted bad press, they drew the conclusion that I was creating problems. The message that was being sent was loud and clear: Why couldn't I just be an RA who went along for the ride and didn't ask questions?

This all took place in July, but remember the months of September, October, November, and December 2020 when Benevento, Wheeler, and I were clashing over the situation involving Charles Munoz? That was July. Then there were the months of September, October, November, and December 2020, when Benevento and Wheeler and I were clashing with regard to San Francisco's groundwater discharge enforcement action issue, which was discussed in the chapter "The EPA versus California" under the discussion "Syringes in the Bay," and the California State Implementation Plan (SIP) issue, which I also discussed in said chapter.

I was told by my R9 staff that in one congressional hearing, Administrator Wheeler was asked by Congressman Scott Peters why he couldn't make transboundary sewage at the border as high a priority issue as his regional administrator had made it. And I was told that Congressman Tom O'Halleran asked him in a different congressional hearing essentially the same thing in regard to the Navajo Nation abandoned uranium mine issue. One thing I am very confident about is, these events didn't help me with my standing in Administrator Wheeler's eyes.

So one thing I know is, I wasn't terminated for the defamatory reasons they stated. Was it one or all these other issues that led to my termination? I have no clue. What I do know is, I did my job; and according to many powers that be, I did it extremely well. I've been told by a very reliable source that HQ was talking to my ultimate replacement months before my termination. That would have been the same time period when I was pushing back with Benevento and telling him I would not disapprove the requested SIPs. I am positive that by Christmas, the decision had been made. It was only a decision as to when to pull the plug.

So the call came the morning of February 5, 2020, the morning after the 2020 State of the Union Address by the president. They wanted my resignation. I told them that if they didn't give me the reason for terminating me, they would have to fire me. They refused to tell me the reason, and I was formally terminated by the EPA at 5:00 p.m. EST.

The Presidential Personnel Office called three weeks later to ask what had happened. I told them, "You tell me." They said they were miffed that Wheeler terminated me and said that I was appointed by the president and that the president wanted me back in the administration. I explained that this was a load off my shoulders and a nice message to my bruised ego after being fired on a national level, but I explained that I was expecting to be hired by a major national law firm. As such, I suggested an appointment as the US representative on the Western Interstate Energy Board. The president appointed me to that board approximately one month after my firing. The pandemic then kicked in, and joining the law firm was delayed until things could return to normal. So where do I go from here?

I am a devout Christian. I often say, "The Lord works in mysterious ways." I often ask the Lord in prayer what Saul asked when he converted on the road to Damascus: "Lord, what do You want me to do (Acts 9:6)?" I prayed that prayer on a daily basis, and then I was appointed to R9 RA. Let's not forget the appointment roller-coaster ride I was on from the NLRB, to the Federal Mediation and Conciliation Service, and finally landing in the EPA.

I have to be honest with you, after the position of the EPA sunk in, I asked God, "Really? The EPA? Why?" Honestly, my image of the EPA might have been like the image many of you have, that they were the gotcha group. Hopefully, as you read through this journey with me, you understood the accomplishments Nixon hoped would happen when he created the EPA by executive order. For me, within months, maybe even weeks, it became very clear why God put me in this position.

I coined a quick phase when people asked, "Hey, how's the job?" My standard line was, "I have the best job in America to help the underprivileged and underserved." And I would usually add, "And the only time this job is frustrating is when it has something to do with DC and EPA headquarters over things I have no control and often are not even made aware of." But those days were far and few in between, and no matter how frustrating those days were, it was well worth it, as I was able to bundle all my past work experience and my conviction to meeting issues head-on in the field, focus on my top priorities, and in the end, be a voice for all of the needs of Region 9.

Upon further reflection, when you consider it, I was terminated just weeks before all of EPA shut down due to COVID-19. Had I not been terminated, I would have been the most miserable RA in the country. To be a virtual RA would have driven me nuts. As a good friend and career R9 staffer told me after my termination, "You only lost a paycheck, and you'll probably make that back several times over with your lawsuit. You would have hated being an RA with the restraints caused by the pandemic, and had you not been fired, you never would have written your book."

Well, true, I did only lose a paycheck, and the verdict is still out as to proceeds from my lawsuit, but this book is a labor of love—not just a love for myself but a love for the people of R9, whom I swore an oath to serve, and also those within R9, whom I served with. But much to my surprise, there ended up being one huge addition to me being fired, underscoring that God works in mysterious ways. Let me explain.

All high-level Trump appointees took the Trump ethics pledge, which extended the prohibition to represent clients for compensation before Congress or federal agencies from one to two years. One week before leaving office, he revoked the pledge, meaning I only had the traditional one-year prohibition. And since I was fired on February 5, 2020, as of February 5, 2021, I am free to represent clients before Congress and federal agencies.[14]

So I am back to asking like Saul: "Lord, what do You want me to do?" Whatever the next mission is, whatever the next chapter in my professional life is, I am good with wherever I end up. I strongly believe that I will find myself back to, in some way, helping my tribes and the Pacific Island territories, helping the people I have truly come to know and love.

In closing, I leave you with another song. While I am a Deadhead and Alan Bacock could not have dedicated a better song for me from the Grateful Dead collection than "Truckin'," the song that really tells the story of my life and is definitely one of my favorites is Frank Sinatra's "My Way." As you read the lyrics to the song, think of the personal story I've told and how it had an impact on me and how I responded.

> And now the end is here, And so I face that final curtain, And so I face the final curtain.
>
> My friend I'll make it clear, I'll state my case, of which I am certain.
>
> I've lived a life that's full, I traveled each and every highway.
>
> And more, much more than this, I did it my way.
>
> Regrets, I've had a few, but then again few to too mention.
>
> I did what I had to do, I saw it through without exemption.

---

[14] On May 1, 2021, I started my new firm, Michael Stoker & Associates, a governmental and public relations firm. So for those of you needing assistance with local, state, or federal agencies, including the US EPA, feel free to contact me at mikestoker1955@gmail.com.

I planned each charted course. Each careful step, along the byway.

And more, much more than this, I did it my way.

Ye, there were times I'm sure you knew, when I bit off more than I could chew.

But through it all, when there was doubt I ate it up and spit it out.

I faced it all and I stood tall and did it my way.

For what is a man, what has he got? If not himself then he has naught.

Not to say the things he truly feels. And not the words of someone who kneels.

Let the record show, I took the blows and did it my way.

As for the job I did as the Region 9 regional administrator, it wasn't my way. It was the way my career staff guided me in identifying the problems and issues that needed to be addressed to serve the EPA mission to protect human health and the environment. Like a detective, you follow the facts. You don't create them. And the causes I took on were only a response to where those facts took me, whether it was the Navajo Nation's abandoned uranium mines, transboundary sewage, Hunters Point, Red Hill, coral reef restoration and protection, or the everyday issues that are often forgotten or neglected in DC.

All that I did every day I woke up as the regional administrator was give 100 percent to serve the EPA and its mission without bias or political indifference. And for that, I have absolutely no regrets whatsoever. Thank you and good luck to all the career staff in Region 9. Thank you for giving me two years to work with the best of the best. *Ciao.*

ABOUT THE AUTHOR

The author is a business, environmental, and agricultural attorney. He has substantial experience in the public sector as well. He was elected and previously served on the Santa Barbara County Board of Supervisors from 1986 to 1994, and he was named in 1993 by *Governing Magazine* as the most valuable public official in county government in America, number one out of 18,789 individuals.

He served as the chairman of the California Agricultural Labor Relations Board from 1995 to 2000, as the California deputy secretary of state from 2000 to 2002, and as the Southwest administrator for the US EPA from 2018 to 2020. The Southwest region represents sixty million people and serves eight time zones from Navajo Nation to the east and the Northern Mariana Islands to the west with American Samoa, Guam, Hawaii, California, Arizona, and Nevada in between.